Ro
Essentials of th
l
Paul Kocourek

MW00412333

Contents

Chapter 1

The book of Romans is a Divinely-inspired masterpiece of teaching about the Christian life, and covers virtually every major Christian doctrine. It is the Christian's go-to handbook for understanding salvation through faith in Jesus Christ. It has been said that a believer who knows Romans thoroughly will never be taken-in by the false doctrines of the cults. It is my hope and prayer that God will be glorified in this work, and that every believer can be free of errors in theology that undercut the salvation that God gives us through His Son Jesus.

Many centuries have passed since the days of the Apostle Paul who heard of Christian believers in the city of Rome. Unable to visit them personally, Paul put down in writing everything he could think of to cover the theology that the baby believers in Rome would need as Christians to know.

We realize today that this was God's intention, so that instead of Paul's teachings being given in person to a small section of believers but otherwise lost to the ages, we have his letter through Divine inspiration carefully preserved through the centuries to teach us today all the essential doctrines we also need to learn.

1 Paul, a servant of Jesus Christ, called to be an apostle, separated unto the gospel of God, 2 (Which he had promised afore by his prophets in the holy scriptures,) (Rom 1:1-2)

Rome was the political capital and greatest city in the world, the very heart of the mightiest empire the world had ever known. Its population was 1 million (though one inscription says 4 million), so it was comparable to major cities in the 21st century. It was a matter of prestige and pride to be able to say that you were a Roman citizen. It was to the believers in mighty Rome that Paul was writing.

The Apostle Paul was himself a natural-born Roman citizen, and that citizenship carried the full weight of the political and military might of Rome.

When Paul was arrested in the city of Jerusalem, the guards of the Roman garrison at Antonia Fortress were going to "examine" him by means of the torture of scourging, but, the revelation of Paul's Roman citizenship frightened the guards.

24 The chief captain commanded him to be brought into the castle, and bade that he should be examined by scourging; that he might know wherefore they cried so against him. 25 And as they bound him with thongs, Paul said unto the centurion that stood by, Is it lawful for you to scourge a man that is a Roman, and uncondemned? 26 When the centurion heard that, he went and told the chief captain, saying, Take heed what thou doest: for this man is a Roman. 27 Then the chief captain came, and said unto him, Tell me, art thou a Roman? He said, Yea. 28 And the chief captain answered, With a great sum obtained I this freedom. And Paul said, But I was free born. 29 Then straightway they departed from him which should have examined him: and the chief captain also was afraid, after he knew that he was a Roman, and because he had bound him. (Acts 22:26-29)

The men were afraid – with good reason -- because they had, even if inadvertently, broken one Roman law, and were about to make an even worse violation! Rome dealt harshly with those that broke its laws, and these men knew it!

Paul had never met the believers in Rome, and they did not know him. In just a few choice statements, Paul starts this lengthy letter by introducing himself. Paul says first about himself is that he is a servant. The Romans knew full well the roles of master and servant, as historical figures suggest that one out of every three people was a slave in Rome. It would have been to them scandalous, if not unthinkable, that someone who was a servant would be writing to instruct them! Yet, his occasion to write to them is not of someone trying to be master over them, but as a servant to Jesus Christ and to them. Nevertheless, he had authority in the Body of Christ, for he was called by Jesus to be an apostle. Paul was separated out to preach the gospel, which means he dropped everything else to follow that calling. He served Jesus whole-heartedly, proud to be a servant to the King of Kings! Paul adds that the gospel was "promised afore by his prophets in the holy scriptures", so his message was not some new spur-of-the-moment, just-now-invented thing. It had the full weight and authority of the Word of God behind it!

3 Concerning his Son Jesus Christ our Lord, which was made of the seed of David according to the flesh; 4 And declared to be the Son of God with power, according to the spirit of holiness, by the resurrection from the dead: 5 By whom we have received grace and apostleship, for obedience to the faith among all nations, for his name: 6 Among whom are ye also the called of Jesus Christ: (Romans 1:3-6)

Having introduced himself, Paul addresses why he was writing to them. It was about Jesus! The believing Roman reader would have relaxed. They would have been glad to hear more about their Savior and Lord, and that from no less than an apostle who said, "our" Lord, not "your" Lord. Paul was in this together with them, a fellow believer. Paul then describes Jesus, first in His humanity as having been descended from King David, but then second in His Resurrection as having been declared the Son of Almighty God with power!

Jesus is 100% man and 100% God!

Romans is the gospel of God's grace, and it gets reflected in Paul's next statement that the apostles received their apostleship from Jesus along with grace as well. Without grace from Jesus, they could not have been apostles, and without grace, we in all the world, wherever we live, cannot be obedient to the faith. Then Paul makes an interesting tie-in for these Romans. Even as he himself was called by Jesus, so were they. All believers are both called by God and are recipients of His grace.

7 To all that be in Rome, beloved of God, called to be saints: Grace to you and peace from God our Father, and the Lord Jesus Christ. 8 First, I thank my God through Jesus Christ for you all, that your faith is spoken of throughout the whole world. 9 For God is my witness, whom I serve with my spirit in the gospel of his Son, that without ceasing I make mention of you always in my prayers; 10 Making request, if by any means now at length I might have a prosperous journey by the will of God to come unto you. 11 For I long to see you, that I

may impart unto you some spiritual gift, to the end ye may be established; 12 That is, that I may be comforted together with you by the mutual faith both of you and me. 13 Now I would not have you ignorant, brethren, that oftentimes I purposed to come unto you, (but was let hitherto,) that I might have some fruit among you also, even as among other Gentiles. (Romans 1:7-13)

Paul now begins his letter with a salutation. They are "beloved of God." Do you and I realize that the Romans had the same sins we deal with in our lives, and when because of our sins we feel brought low and ashamed and wonder whether God still loves us, that we are actually and truly, "beloved of God"? Yes, like the Romans, you and I who believe in Jesus Christ are also beloved of God! Then Paul says of the Romans (and by extension, he says of you and me), that they are saints. Now, I grew up in a tradition that believed that saints are superstars of the faith, people of such high and exemplary life, that a church council would declare them to be saints. This is contrary to the Word of God, which calls ALL believers saints, and not by some council's decree.

Then Paul tells them the familiar Christian "grace and peace" greeting found in nearly all the epistles (see Rom 1:7; 1 Cor 1:3; 2 Cor 1:2; Gal 1:3; Eph 1:2; Phil 1:2; Col 1:2; 1 Thes 1:1; 2 Thes 1:2; 1 Tim 1:2; 2 Tim 1:2; Titus 1:4; Philemon 3; Heb 13:25; 1 Pet 1:2; 2 Pet 1:2; 2 John 3; 3 John 15; Jude 2). I was taught that the greeting is a combination of Greek and Hebrew cultures. The Greeks greeted each other with grace, while the Hebrews greeted then (and still do today) each other with "shalom", which means "peace". The Church is a blend of Jew and Gentile, and the greeting reflects this. Both God the Father and our Lord Jesus Christ are both lovingly blessing us with grace and peace.

Next Paul give thanks for them. Though he has not met them, yet their faith is known worldwide! Now, how did this vibrant community get started in Rome in the first place? For the answer, we need only look to the book of Acts on Pentecost Sunday. Pentecost, also called the Feast of Weeks, was a big Jewish holy day, and people – both natural bloodline Jews and Gentile proselyte converts – from all around the Roman Empire were present to celebrate it. The Holy Spirit fell on all the disciples, giving them to speak with the languages of all the many people represented there:

5 And there were dwelling at Jerusalem Jews, devout men, out of every nation under heaven. 6 Now when this was noised abroad, the multitude came together, and were confounded, because that every man heard them speak in his own language. 7 And they were all amazed and marvelled, saying one to another, Behold, are not all these which speak Galilaeans? 8 And how hear we every man in our own tongue, wherein we were born? 9 Parthians, and Medes, and Elamites, and the dwellers in Mesopotamia, and in Judaea, and Cappadocia, in Pontus, and Asia, 10 Phrygia, and Pamphylia, in Egypt, and in the parts of Libya about Cyrene, and strangers of Rome, Jews and proselytes (Acts 2:5-10)

Notice at the end of the list "strangers of Rome, Jews and proselytes". Yes, those from Rome heard the salvation message proclaimed by Peter, and having believed in Jesus (Acts 2:31-36), they returned back to Rome to excitedly tell all their friends and neighbors, everyone they knew, about their new faith in Jesus. That community grew and grew, until it was talked about everywhere, and even Paul finally heard about it. He was no doubt immensely encouraged, and was so thankful for this thriving community of believers about whom he had heard, and he prayed faithfully for them; he wanted so much that that God would grant him to go visit them to teach them, to fill in the missing details of the faith that they would not have gotten through Peter and their Old Testament Bibles. However, he couldn't, and so great was his concern for their need for spiritual growth, that he wrote the long letter to them at Rome to give them all the essential doctrines they would need to know as Christians.

His letter was his long-distance teaching, his spiritual gift to them (not the same as a spiritual gift, which he addresses later in Romans 12), and his purpose was to see them grow in their faith and be "established", that is, so they would be rooted and grounded in the faith, and not swayed or deceived by false doctrine. Paul wrote of this also to the believers at Ephesus:

14 That we henceforth be no more children, tossed to and fro, and carried about with every wind of doctrine, by the sleight of men, and cunning craftiness, whereby they lie in wait to deceive; 15 But speaking the truth in love, may grow up into him in all things, which is the head, even Christ (Eph 4:14-15)

Finally, it was in God's providence that Paul was prevented to go visit the Romans in person at that time, because that by Paul writing that letter to the Romans, God through Paul was giving you and me that same instruction as well in order to give us all the essential doctrines we would need to know as Christians.

14 I am debtor both to the Greeks, and to the Barbarians; both to the wise, and to the unwise. 15 So, as much as in me is, I am ready to preach the gospel to you that are at Rome also. (Rom 1:14-15)

Paul thought of himself as being obligated to preach the gospel, so much so, that he considers it a debt he owed. He wanted to preach it to the Greeks (the wise) and the Barbarians (the unwise).With that drive and passion, he wanted also to preach to the people at Rome. The question is: why? What was the motivation, the unquenchable thirst that drove him to want to be preaching to so many people at every stratum of society in all walks of life? He revealed the answer to those questions in the following key passage of the book of Romans.

16 For I am not ashamed of the gospel of Christ: for it is the power of God unto salvation to every one that believeth; to the Jew first, and also to the Greek. 17 For therein is the righteousness of God revealed from faith to faith: as it is written, The just shall live by faith. (Rom 1:16-17)

This passage is a pivotal one summing up the entire letter, the anchor and cornerstone upon which the rest of the letter rests. Let us look at it in detail then.

"I am not ashamed..." Shame is what we experience when we have done something wrong, or have support for something wrong.
"of the gospel of Christ". The gospel is all about Jesus Christ
"for it is the power of God" There is power in the gospel to affect change in human hearts

"unto salvation" That power is for our salvation

"to every one that believeth" That gospel power is acquired simply through faith

"to the Jew first, and also to the Greek". The first people to be saved were Jews present in Jerusalem for the Feast of Weeks, i.e. Pentecost (Acts 2). Those Jews were the first people to be saved by faith in Jesus. But the gospel is not restricted to Jews. It is also for Gentiles. We see the first Gentiles to be saved with Cornelius and his household (Acts 10).

"For therein" means, in the gospel message itself

"is the righteousness of God revealed". The gospel reveals God's righteousness. Why is that important? As we will see later in Romans, it means that God, the righteous, revealed a way we, the unrighteous, could be acceptable to Him without His compromising His own righteousness. He does not merely have a standard, but He Himself IS the standard!

"from faith to faith: as it is written, The just shall live by faith" The way to God is by faith. The "from faith to faith" can be said this way, "from start to finish." We start our journey with God with faith, and we go through all of life to the end, and it is always by faith. We LIVE by faith, from start to finish!

So, why do we need the gospel, anyway? Paul begins to address three groups of people.

First, he addresses the "barbarians" whom he called "unwise" in vs 14 where he wrote, "…and to the Barbarians; … to the unwise."

Because God is righteous, He cannot bear unrighteousness. Sins are acts of high-treason. They incur God's wrath, and that is a truly fearful place to be. The frightfulness of this dilemma was expounded by Reverend Jonathan Edwards in his classic sermon, "Sinners in the Hands of An Angry God" a sermon he preached at Enfield, July 8th, 1741, where he said:

[Quote]
The observation from the words that I would now insist upon is this.—"There is nothing that keeps wicked men at any one moment out of hell, but the mere pleasure of God."—By the mere pleasure of God, I mean his sovereign pleasure, his arbitrary will, restrained by no obligation, hindered by no manner of difficulty, any more than if nothing else but God's mere will had in the least degree, or in any respect whatsoever, any hand in the preservation of wicked men one moment.—The truth of this observation may appear by the following considerations.

1. There is no want of power in God to cast wicked men into hell at any moment. Men's hands cannot be strong when God rises up. The strongest have no power to resist him, nor can any deliver out of his hands.—He is not only able to cast wicked men into hell, but he can most easily do it. Sometimes an earthly prince meets with a great deal of difficulty to subdue a rebel, who has found means to fortify himself, and has made himself strong by the numbers of his followers. But it is not so with God. There is no fortress that is any defense from the power of God. Though hand join in hand, and vast multitudes of God's enemies combine and associate themselves, they are easily broken in pieces. They are as great heaps of light chaff before the whirlwind; or large quantities of dry stubble before devouring flames. We find it easy to tread on and crush a worm that we see crawling on the earth; so it is easy for us to cut or singe a

slender thread that any thing hangs by: thus easy is it for God, when he pleases, to cast his enemies down to hell. What are we, that we should think to stand before him, at whose rebuke the earth trembles, and before whom the rocks are thrown down?

2. They deserve to be cast into hell; so that divine justice never stands in the way, it makes no objection against God's using his power at any moment to destroy them. Yea, on the contrary, justice calls aloud for an infinite punishment of their sins. Divine justice says of the tree that brings forth such grapes of Sodom, "Cut it down, why cumbereth it the ground?" Luke 13:7. The sword of divine justice is every moment brandished over their heads, and it is nothing but the hand of arbitrary mercy, and God's mere will, that holds it back.

3. They are already under a sentence of condemnation to hell. They do not only justly deserve to be cast down thither, but the sentence of the law of God, that eternal and immutable rule of righteousness that God has fixed between him and mankind, is gone out against them, and stands against them; so that they are bound over already to hell. "He that believeth not is condemned already. "(John 3:18) So that every unconverted man properly belongs to hell; that is his place; from thence he is, John 8:23. "Ye are from beneath," and thither he is bound; it is the place that justice, and God's word, and the sentence of his unchangeable law, assign to him.

4. They are now the objects of that very same anger and wrath of God, that is expressed in the torments of hell. And the reason why they do not go down to hell at each moment, is not because God, in whose power they are, is not then very angry with them; as he is with many miserable creatures now tormented in hell, who there feel and bear the fierceness of

his wrath. Yea, God is a great deal more angry with great numbers that are now on earth; yea, doubtless, with many that are now in this congregation, who it may be are at ease, than he is with many of those who are now in the flames of hell.—So that it is not because God is unmindful of their wickedness, and does not resent it, that he does not let loose his hand and cut them off. God is not altogether such an one as themselves, though they may imagine him to be so. The wrath of God burns against them, their damnation does not slumber; the pit is prepared, the fire is made ready, the furnace is now hot, ready to receive them; the flames do now rage and glow. The glittering sword is whet, and held over them, and the pit hath opened its mouth under them. [Unquote]

With these words in mind, let us read Paul's condemnation of the ungodly, the "barbarians" (what we might also call pagans or the heathen).

18 For the wrath of God is revealed from heaven against all ungodliness and unrighteousness of men, who hold the truth in unrighteousness; 19 Because that which may be known of God is manifest in them; for God hath shewed it unto them. (Rom 1:18-19)

It said that they "hold the truth". It means they hold back the truth, that is, they suppress it. They don't want to hear about the truth, even though they do actually know the truth. Why are we confident they know about it? Because God has shown to them. Scripture says, "The fool hath said in his heart, There is no God. They are corrupt, they have done abominable works, there is none that doeth good" (Psalm 14:1)

The Universe around us demonstrates that there is a God. Those who believe in a literal Creation point out that just as a fine-tuned watch did not come together randomly on its own, but was designed by a Master Craftsman, so too is the Universe one gigantic fine-tuned watch that was created by a Master Craftsman.

20 For the invisible things of him from the creation of the world are clearly seen, being understood by the things that are made, even his eternal power and Godhead; so that they are without excuse (Rom 1:20)

The problem with people is that they do not WANT to honor God because they love the darkness.
19 And this is the condemnation, that light is come into the world, and men loved darkness rather than light, because their deeds were evil. (John 3:19)

But, despite their willful rejection of God, there is still in Mankind's innermost being the knowledge of God. Not able to totally eradicate that knowledge, men have made substitutes more acceptable to their way of thinking. They chose to make gods out of things they see in the Creation. When people do that, they step out of the light into darkness, and how great is that darkness of the heart!

21 Because that, when they knew God, they glorified him not as God, neither were thankful; but became vain in their imaginations, and their foolish heart was darkened. 22 Professing themselves to be wise, they became fools, 23 And changed the glory of the uncorruptible God into an image made like to corruptible man, and to birds, and

fourfooted beasts, and creeping things. (Rom 1:21-23)

When people so totally turn their back on God, He gives them over to the folly of their deep dark sins. Three times it tells us that God gave them up.

24 Wherefore God also gave them up to uncleanness through the lusts of their own hearts, to dishonour their own bodies between themselves: 25 Who changed the truth of God into a lie, and worshipped and served the creature more than the Creator, who is blessed for ever. Amen. (Rom 1:24-25)

The long list of sinfulness starts with what seems such a minor thing: "neither were thankful." A lack of thankfulness lies at the start of the long decline away from God! In contrast, for the believer, the giving of thanks is a wonderful thing. When we pray, we are reminded to thank God when we present our prayers and supplications.

6 Be careful for nothing; but in every thing by prayer and supplication with thanksgiving let your requests be made known unto God. (Phil 4:6)

Paul continues describing the long decline away from God, telling how God gave such people up to debase themselves with lesbianism and homosexuality, which God calls "vile affections" and a "reprobate mind", the latter being a mind that no longer can discern between good and evil. Their sins have seared their conscience like a branding iron burns a permanent scarring mark into the leather hide of cattle.

26 For this cause God gave them up unto vile affections:

for even their women did change the natural use into that which is against nature: 27 And likewise also the men, leaving the natural use of the woman, burned in their lust one toward another; men with men working that which is unseemly, and receiving in themselves that recompence of their error which was meet. 28 And even as they did not like to retain God in their knowledge, God gave them over to a reprobate mind, to do those things which are not convenient (Rom 1:26-28)

The Bible teaches there are three categories of sin.

16 For all that is in the world, the lust of the flesh, and the lust of the eyes, and the pride of life, is not of the Father, but is of the world. (1 John 2:16)

1. the lust of the flesh (satisfying the illicit cravings of our bodies)
2. the lust of the eyes (desire for material possessions, coveting things we see)
3. the pride of life (the thirst of proud self-importance, power, and position)

The following list of sins given by the inspiration of the Holy Spirit through Paul runs the gamut of all three categories of sin.

29 Being filled with all unrighteousness, fornication, wickedness, covetousness, maliciousness; full of envy, murder, debate, deceit, malignity; whisperers, 30 Backbiters, haters of God, despiteful, proud, boasters, inventors of evil things, disobedient to parents, 31 Without understanding, covenantbreakers, without

natural affection, implacable, unmerciful: 32 Who knowing the judgment of God, that they which commit such things are worthy of death, not only do the same, but have pleasure in them that do them. (Rom 1:29-32)

The conclusion is that the "barbarians", these "heathen", are utterly guilty and lost in their sin.

They need a Savior to bring salvation, which is gloriously available to all if they will but believe the gospel of God's salvation by grace through faith.

Chapter 2

In Chapter 1, we saw that Paul began describing the reasons the human race needs salvation. In this chapter, he will continue with two more groups of people who are guilty, and therefore also need salvation. Paul had written, "I am debtor both to the Greeks, and to the Barbarians; both to the wise, and to the unwise." In chapter 1, he addressed the "barbarians" who are "unwise." Now he addresses the Greeks, who are the "wise". The Greeks were indeed thirsty for wisdom, as Paul noted:

22 For the Jews require a sign, and the Greeks seek after wisdom: (1 Cor 1:22)

The Greeks produced classic philosophers like Socrates, Plato, and Aristotle, so yes, they indeed sought after wisdom. Now in the book of Romans, as Paul first addressed the "unwise" barbarians, we can imagine the "wise" Greeks nodding their heads and agreeing that the "unwise" barbarians were horrible in their sinfulness.

However, the "wise" Greeks get no exemption from God's judgment, for Paul at this point turns the attention on them. Even as the "wise" Greeks agree with passing judgment on the "unwise" barbarians, they unwittingly end up passing judgment on themselves because they were guilty of doing the same sinful things for which they were condemning the barbarians!

1 Therefore thou art inexcusable, O man, whosoever thou art that judgest: for wherein thou judgest another, thou condemnest thyself; for thou that judgest doest the

same things. 2 But we are sure that the judgment of God is according to truth against them which commit such things. 3 And thinkest thou this, O man, that judgest them which do such things, and doest the same, that thou shalt escape the judgment of God? (Romans 2:1-3)

No, there is no escaping the judgment of God for sin committed. For even the Christian believer, judgment and wrath are not escaped. Rather, they are, if we can say it this way, "redirected", as in the judgment and wrath for the believer's sins has been poured out, not on the believer, but on Jesus on the cross in lieu of the believer.

So, if no one escapes the judgment of God, why has that judgment not already been poured out? Why has God not smitten us already in Divine fury and wrath? The answer is rich and deep. God has not already vented His wrath because in addition to being a God of holy justice, He is also a God of kindness. He shows us kindness in order to lead us to repentance so that He won't have to judge us.

4 Or despisest thou the riches of his goodness and forbearance and longsuffering; not knowing that the goodness of God leadeth thee to repentance? (Romans 2:4)

God has not "blown us away" yet because of His goodness and kindness. He doesn't want to have to vent His wrath on us because He wants to save us. Why? Because He LOVES us! People sometimes make the foolish mistake of thinking that if God does not immediately vent Divine wrath, then it means He is not going to do so at all. But, remember this:

Wrath delayed is NOT wrath denied!

When people think God's mercy in not smiting us right
away is a sign that He won't ever do so, they therefore
harden their hearts to go on sinning. In doing so, they are
storing up terrible wrath for themselves. God sees
everything we do, and keeps very good records.

**5 But after thy hardness and impenitent heart treasurest
up unto thyself wrath against the day of wrath and
revelation of the righteous judgment of God; 6 Who will
render to every man according to his deeds: (Romans
2:5-6)**

The following verses seem to say that if we continually live
a good life, then we will get to Heaven, whereas if we sin,
we go to Hell. That is actually true as far as it goes, applying
equally to Jew or Gentile, for with God "there is no respect
of persons with God". BUT! Here is the problem: not one of
us practices "patient continuance in well doing" to receive
"glory, honour, and peace, to every man that worketh good."
We "do not obey the truth, but obey unrighteousness."
Instead, we all, whether Jew or Gentile, are accruing to
ourselves "indignation and wrath, tribulation and anguish,
upon every soul of man that doeth evil."

**7 To them who by patient continuance in well doing seek
for glory and honour and immortality eternal life: 8 But
unto them that are contentious, and do not obey the
truth, but obey unrighteousness, indignation and wrath,
9 Tribulation and anguish, upon every soul of man that
doeth evil, of the Jew first, and also of the Gentile; 10
But glory, honour, and peace, to every man that worketh**

good, to the Jew first, and also to the Gentile: 11 For there is no respect of persons with God. (Romans 2:7-11)

The Jew, upon reading the letter of Romans up to this point, might begin to feel a little uncomfortable, but then stifle that discomfort and dismiss it. After all, are they not God's chosen people to whom He gave the Law through Moses? You see, the Jews had three foundational points they believed exempted them from God's judgment, and they prided themselves on those three points:

1) They had the Law
2) They were circumcised
3) They were descendants of God's friend, Abraham

Paul therefore sets about dispelling their illusions on those three points to demonstrate their guilt as Jews also. Paul tells them that if a Gentile sins without having the Law, he is no less condemned than a Jew who has the Law, but disobeys it.

12 For as many as have sinned without law shall also perish without law: and as many as have sinned in the law shall be judged by the law; 13 (For not the hearers of the law are just before God, but the doers of the law shall be justified. 14 For when the Gentiles, which have not the law, do by nature the things contained in the law, these, having not the law, are a law unto themselves: 15 Which shew the work of the law written in their hearts, their conscience also bearing witness, and their thoughts the mean while accusing or else excusing one another;) (Rom 2:12-15)

People sometimes think that if a sin is hidden in secret, no one will know. Yet, Scripture says otherwise:

12 For the word of God is quick, and powerful, and sharper than any twoedged sword, piercing even to the dividing asunder of soul and spirit, and of the joints and marrow, and is a discerner of the thoughts and intents of the heart. 13 Neither is there any creature that is not manifest in his sight: but all things are naked and opened unto the eyes of him with whom we have to do. (Hebrews 4:12-13)

God's Word penetrates to the very heart and core of our being and reveals our very thoughts. In the Day of Judgment, all the secrets men would try to hide will be revealed and judged by Jesus Himself. How so? By "According to my gospel". The gospel Paul preached (Rom 1:16-17) is that salvation is available to all who believe in Jesus Christ.

16 In the day when God shall judge the secrets of men by Jesus Christ according to my gospel. (Romans 2:16)

Now Paul focuses hard on the Jews in particular. He starts demonstrating that their boast in the Law doesn't protect them from judgment. Paul himself was a Pharisee that was extremely meticulous about being law-conscious. He referred to himself this way:

6 But when Paul perceived that the one part were Sadducees, and the other Pharisees, he cried out in the council, Men and brethren, I am a Pharisee, the son of a Pharisee: of the hope and resurrection of the dead I am called in question. (Acts 23:5)

So, he knew full well just how Jews thought of themselves.

17 Behold, thou art called a Jew, and restest in the law, and makest thy boast of God, 18 And knowest his will, and approvest the things that are more excellent, being instructed out of the law; 19 And art confident that thou thyself art a guide of the blind, a light of them which are in darkness, 20 An instructor of the foolish, a teacher of babes, which hast the form of knowledge and of the truth in the law. 21 Thou therefore which teachest another, teachest thou not thyself? thou that preachest a man should not steal, dost thou steal? 22 Thou that sayest a man should not commit adultery, dost thou commit adultery? thou that abhorrest idols, dost thou commit sacrilege? 23 Thou that makest thy boast of the law, through breaking the law dishonourest thou God? 24 For the name of God is blasphemed among the Gentiles through you, as it is written. (Romans 2:17-24)

After showing how the Law does not exempt them, now he addresses how circumcision does not exempt them either. Circumcision was given as a sign that a person was covered by the contract with God which is the Law. So, breaking the Law breaks circumcision.

25 For circumcision verily profiteth, if thou keep the law: but if thou be a breaker of the law, thy circumcision is made uncircumcision. 26 Therefore if the uncircumcision keep the righteousness of the law, shall not his uncircumcision be counted for circumcision? 27 And shall not uncircumcision which is by nature, if it fulfil the law, judge thee, who by the letter and

circumcision dost transgress the law? (Romans 2:25-27)

John the Baptist addressed this pride the Jews had in being descendants of Abraham:

9 And think not to say within yourselves, We have Abraham to our father: for I say unto you, that God is able of these stones to raise up children unto Abraham. (Matt 3:9)

Now Paul goes after the third foundation the Jews depended upon to be exempted from God's judgment, that they are descendants from Abraham after the flesh.

28 For he is not a Jew, which is one outwardly; neither is that circumcision, which is outward in the flesh: 29 But he is a Jew, which is one inwardly; and circumcision is that of the heart, in the spirit, and not in the letter; whose praise is not of men, but of God. (Rom 2:28-29)

For Jew or Gentile, it is not our outward obedience, nor dependence upon the Law, nor circumcision, nor being a descendant of Abraham, that is required by God. Heaven cannot be attained by anything we do because we are all guilty, Jew and Gentile alike. We need a Savior to do for us what we cannot do for ourselves. Jesus Christ alone can fulfill the righteousness that God requires of us all.

Chapter 3

Some of the people present in Jerusalem on the day of the Feast of Weeks, aka Pentecost, were from Rome. They were there to celebrate that Jewish Feast day because they were either Jews themselves, or proselyte Jews (i.e. Gentiles who converted to the God of Abraham, Isaac, and Jacob). We see this at the end of verse 10 below.

8 And how hear we every man in our own tongue, wherein we were born? 9 Parthians, and Medes, and Elamites, and the dwellers in Mesopotamia, and in Judaea, and Cappadocia, in Pontus, and Asia, 10 Phrygia, and Pamphylia, in Egypt, and in the parts of Libya about Cyrene, and strangers of Rome, Jews and proselytes (Acts 2:8-10)

They got saved at Peter's preaching on Pentecost and returned to Rome, sharing and spreading the Good News to all their families, friends and neighbors, which is how the church in Rome grew and grew until Paul himself heard about them. Now in chapter 3, Paul addresses what must have been a possible sore point for Jews in Rome who were not believers in Messiah Jesus (but maybe knew Jews who were saved). Paul previously demonstrated that the barbarians (the "unwise"), the Greeks (the "wise"), and the Jews were all accounted guilty before God, and that the Jews in particular didn't get "a free pass" because of being descendants of Abraham and circumcised. In this chapter, Paul anticipates objections that might be raised to try to find a "loophole", some point or other that might exempt them as Jews from being liable to God's judgment, and then answers those objections.

Objection 1. If Jews get judged along with the despised Gentiles, then what is the point of being a Jew?

1 What advantage then hath the Jew? or what profit is there of circumcision? (Rom 3:1)

The answer follows in the next verse. They were given a true privilege – among all the peoples of the world, they were entrusted with God's Word!

2 Much every way: chiefly, because that unto them were committed the oracles of God. (Rom 3:2)

Objection 2. And, even if some Jews did not believe, Paul tells them that it did not invalidate the truth of God's Word. God is true even if everybody else tells lies.

3 For what if some did not believe? shall their unbelief make the faith of God without effect? 4 God forbid: yea, let God be true, but every man a liar; as it is written, That thou mightest be justified in thy sayings, and mightest overcome when thou art judged. (Rom 3:3-4)

Objection 3. Well, my unrighteousness gives glory to God's own righteousness. That means I am giving glory to God, so why should He judge me? Wouldn't that make God wrong to take vengeance? The answer is, No! God forbid saying such a thing!

5 But if our unrighteousness commend the righteousness of God, what shall we say? Is God unrighteous who taketh vengeance? (I speak as a man) 6 God forbid: for

then how shall God judge the world? (Rom 3:5-6)

Objection 4. Well, yes, I may have told a lie, but it just shows how wonderful God's truth is, so I should be exempted! Paul's answer (and through him, the Holy Spirit's answer) is sharp.

7 For if the truth of God hath more abounded through my lie unto his glory; why yet am I also judged as a sinner? 8 And not rather, (as we be slanderously reported, and as some affirm that we say,) Let us do evil, that good may come? whose damnation is just. (Rom 3:7-8)

Then Paul, speaking as a Jew himself, addresses his fellow Jews. "Are we Jews better than the Gentiles?" The answer is a loud and clear, No! He then cites many Scripture verses that show the condemnation against ALL sinners, Jew or Gentile.

9 What then? are we better than they? No, in no wise: for we have before proved both Jews and Gentiles, that they are all under sin; 10 As it is written, There is none righteous, no, not one: 11 There is none that understandeth, there is none that seeketh after God. 12 They are all gone out of the way, they are together become unprofitable; there is none that doeth good, no, not one. 13 Their throat is an open sepulchre; with their tongues they have used deceit; the poison of asps is under their lips: 14 Whose mouth is full of cursing and bitterness: 15 Their feet are swift to shed blood: 16 Destruction and misery are in their ways: 17 And the way of peace have they not known: 18 There is no fear of

God before their eyes. (Rom 3:9-17)

Now Paul speaks as a Jew to his fellow Jews, concluding the truth about the very Law which the Jews wanted to use as an excuse and exemption from God's judgment.

19 Now we know that what things soever the law saith, it saith to them who are under the law: that every mouth may be stopped, and all the world may become guilty before God. 20 Therefore by the deeds of the law there shall no flesh be justified in his sight: for by the law is the knowledge of sin. (Rom 3:19-20)

We are guilty, every one of us, no exemptions. The entire world is guilty before God, whether Jew or Gentile, whether wise or unwise, whether Greek or barbarian. Paul has shown us that:
1) We're all guilty.
2) We're all going to be judged.
3) We're all going to suffer God's vengeance.

Now, if that was where Paul was going to leave us, it would be a truly sad, desperate, hopeless and helpless situation in which we would find ourselves, with no way out.

However, instead of leaving us in despair, Paul gives a reason to REJOICE! We already know God is righteous, but in this following passage we find the reason to rejoice, For God is solving our unrighteousness problem by placing His OWN righteousness upon us, making us be counted in His eyes as being as righteous as He is!

21 But now the righteousness of God without the law is

manifested, being witnessed by the law and the prophets; 22 Even the righteousness of God which is by faith of Jesus Christ unto all and upon all them that believe: for there is no difference: (Rom 3:21-22)

Read the verses above again. The Jews were trying to achieve the righteousness of God through obedience to the Law of God given through Moses, but were utter failures to achieve that righteousness. Now God is bringing righteousness APART from the bounds of the Law, a righteousness that did NOT depend on the Law and obeying commandments! It should shake us to our core! What's more, though that righteousness is being made available apart from having to obey the Law, yet "the law and the prophets" give witness to it as being true. This is consistent with Scripture that says truth is established by two or three witnesses.

1 This is the third time I am coming to you. In the mouth of two or three witnesses shall every word be established. (2 Cor 13:1)

So, this righteousness of God (apart from Law-keeping) is shown to be solidly true by "the mouth" of two solid witnesses, the Law and the Prophets! What's different, is that this righteousness being spoken of does not come by trying to keep the commandments of the Law, but instead it comes by faith. Moreover, it is available to ALL people, Jew or Gentile, wise or unwise, Greek or Barbarian! It is available to people in the Americas, to people in Europe and Asia, to people in Africa and Australia, and to people in every corner of the world including the most remote locations in every continent and in every island!

Read it again: Even the righteousness of God which is by faith of Jesus Christ unto all and upon all them that believe.

This righteousness, which God makes available to us, is by faith in Jesus Christ. Moreover, that righteousness is "unto" all (as in God giving it), and "upon all" (as in covering us thoroughly). The one and only requirement is that it is for "them that believe."

Friends, do we really grasp what this is saying? When people, no matter how utterly sinful, believe in Jesus Christ, they are covered in God's righteousness! In God's eyes, they are as absolutely righteous . . . as He Himself is!

How righteous is God? Let's just say, it doesn't get any better. And that is how righteous a believer in Jesus is regarded by God the Father. The believer's righteousness is that of God Himself.

There has never been a greater generosity than that of God, raising us from the status of utterly deplorable and wicked sinners, to that of saints standing in perfect righteousness. As the next verse reminds us, we have ALL sinned, every last one of us.

23 For all have sinned, and come short of the glory of God (Rom 3:23)

And so, because we have ALL sinned and are utterly bankrupt and unable to save ourselves, God FREELY redeems us by His grace. He buys us back out of our lostness, our helplessness, our hopelessness, through His grace revealed by our faith in Jesus Christ! To "justify" means to declare righteous.

24 Being justified freely by his grace through the redemption that is in Christ Jesus: (Rom 3:24)

So, perhaps some among us might feel like saying it sounds a bit too much like "too good to be true." It's great that God is doing this, but "what's the catch?" After all, how is it possible for God to offer this righteousness? I mean, isn't He required by His own holiness and justice to judge us for our sins? Is He just going to "look the other way"? Not that we want to be judged, but how can He not judge us after showing us how guilty we are? The answer is in the word "propitiation," which is what Jesus is.

25 Whom God hath set forth to be a propitiation through faith in his blood, to declare his righteousness for the remission of sins that are past, through the forbearance of God; 26 To declare, I say, at this time his righteousness: that he might be just, and the justifier of him which believeth in Jesus. (Rom 3:25-26)

It will make matters easier if we understand "propitiation." It means a sacrifice that makes an atonement that satisfies an offended person. Our sins are an unspeakable offense to God. The only satisfaction He can accept is death for the ones committing sins. This is where Jesus comes in. We all deserved death for our sins. Jesus went to the cross in our place and died in our place. The death we deserved, He got.

Someone has said it this way:
Jesus got what He did not deserve (death)

So we could get what we don't deserve (life).

In an Old Testament prophecy, Isaiah 53 prophesies the suffering and death of Jesus on the cross. Here is the passage:

11 He shall see of the travail of his soul, and shall be satisfied: by his knowledge shall my righteous servant justify many; for he shall bear their iniquities. (Isa 53:11)

Let's add identification in this passage:

11 He [God the Father] shall see of the travail of his soul [Jesus], and shall be satisfied: by his knowledge shall my righteous servant justify many; for he shall bear their iniquities.

God the Father saw the "travail", meaning the suffering and agony, of Jesus on the cross, bearing the awesome and awful weight of all our sins as He bore "our iniquities." The Father saw that travail, and as Jesus breathed His last, the Father was satisfied. Everything that outraged Holiness required by way of Divine Justice, Retribution and Wrath, was now fully SATISFIED! Jesus did for us what we could never do—He satisfied God's Wrath.

Backing up to verse 25, it says, "to declare his righteousness for the remission of sins that are past, through the forbearance of God" God held off punishing people in the Old Testament for their sins; instead of meting out punishment, He let people go unpunished, that is, He gave them remission for those sins of the past. He could righteously let them go free because He knew that Jesus was coming later to make the necessary atonement that would satisfy Divine Wrath. With the propitiation that Jesus made, God is shown (vs 26) to be both "just", in that sins were finally and fully punished, and also a "justifier" of believers in Jesus, as in being the One who could forgive those sins and declare the believer in Jesus, though otherwise wicked and sinful, to be fully righteous in His eyes.

With us being recipients of such an amazing display of grace and mercy, dare we brag and boast about how wonderful we have been, and how good we have behaved ourselves? God forbid! We are saved, not by our works (by which we might have boasted), but simply by faith (apart from any deeds of the Law).

27 Where is boasting then? It is excluded. By what law? of works? Nay: but by the law of faith. 28 Therefore we conclude that a man is justified by faith without the deeds of the law. (Rom 3:27-28)

This forgiveness and gift of all-encompassing righteousness, which is of God Himself, is available both to Jew and Gentile alike, yes, to everyone. The law consisting of God's commandments is not null and void. Rather, the fact that our sins and iniquities were FULLY punished through the death of Jesus on the cross, shows the Law has been vindicated. The Law says, Do this or die. We didn't do it. Therefore, we had to die.

God's justice was manifested in that our sins were punished by death.
God's mercy was manifested in that we were not the ones to pay that price.

God's grace was manifested when Jesus died on the cross for those sins on our behalf.

God justifies Jews (the circumcision) and God also justifies Gentiles (non-Jews, the uncircumcision), solely on the basis of faith in Jesus Christ. This does not violate the Law with all its commandments. Rather, it confirms the Law is true and correct because the penalty the Law demanded for disobedience to the commandments (which includes the famous Ten Commandments) has been paid fully by Jesus Christ's shed blood and death on the cross.

29 Is he the God of the Jews only? is he not also of the Gentiles? Yes, of the Gentiles also: 30 Seeing it is one God, which shall justify the circumcision by faith, and uncircumcision through faith. 31 Do we then make void the law through faith? God forbid: yea, we establish the law. (Rom 3:29-30)

What an amazing God we serve! There is no one else like Him!

Chapter 4

1 What shall we say then that Abraham our father, as pertaining to the flesh, hath found? 2 For if Abraham were justified by works, he hath whereof to glory; but not before God. 3 For what saith the scripture? Abraham believed God, and it was counted unto him for righteousness. (Rom 4:1-3)

In chapter 3, we saw that the righteousness from God for believers in Jesus Christ is "being witnessed by the law and the prophets" (Rom 3:21). This provision of having two witnesses is consistent with Scripture that says truth is established by two or three witnesses. Paul quoted the Old Testament as he wrote to the Corinthians:

15 One witness shall not rise up against a man for any iniquity, or for any sin, in any sin that he sinneth: at the mouth of two witnesses, or at the mouth of three witnesses, shall the matter be established. (Deut 19:15)

1 This is the third time I am coming to you. In the mouth of two or three witnesses shall every word be established. (2 Cor 13:1)

Now, it is all very well and good to claim that the Law and Prophets are two witnesses to this righteousness from God apart from the Law, but what proof is there for this claim? Was Paul just making things up from out of his own imagination, or was there really corroboration from the Scriptures?

To answer this vital question, Paul under the inspiration of the Holy Spirit addresses this matter. Paul first cites Abraham for the testimony of the Law.

In Genesis (part of the Pentateuch, aka the Torah) we find God counting Abram (later renamed Abraham) as righteous:

6 And he believed in the LORD; and he counted it to him for righteousness. (Gen 15:6)

Abram had done nothing by way of works. He heard what God said to him, and he believed God; yet, that was good enough for God. God was pleased and glorified that a sinful man believed Him. Abraham's kind of faith was a saving faith. Paul elaborates on the implications of this kind of faith:

4 Now to him that worketh is the reward not reckoned of grace, but of debt. 5 But to him that worketh not, but believeth on him that justifieth the ungodly, his faith is counted for righteousness. (Rom 4:4-5)

Starting with Abraham's faith as our model, Paul points out a general truth about works versus faith. Works get a reward based on what was done. We saw earlier in Romans 2 that we basically get what we deserve.

8 But unto them that are contentious, and do not obey the truth, but obey unrighteousness, indignation and wrath, 9 Tribulation and anguish, upon every soul of man that doeth evil, of the Jew first, and also of the Gentile (Rom 2:8-9)

Our problem is that because of our sins, we deserve nothing good from God, only death.

BUT! If we do not try to approach God based on the works we have done (which are evil), but instead simply "believeth on him that justifieth the ungodly", then it is said of us that, "his faith is counted for righteousness". If instead of trying to approach God by works, if we instead are people who "worketh not", but believe God, our faith is credited for righteousness the same as Abraham's faith was credited for righteousness. Thus, the Law demonstrates there is a righteousness that is credited without works.

Just as Paul cited Abraham for the testimony of the Law, he then cites David for the testimony of the prophets (Psalm 22 prophesied the crucifixion).

6 Even as David also describeth the blessedness of the man, unto whom God imputeth righteousness without works, 7 Saying, Blessed are they whose iniquities are forgiven, and whose sins are covered. 8 Blessed is the man to whom the Lord will not impute sin. (Rom 4:6-8)

In this Church Age of Grace, we are indeed described by verse 8 above: "Blessed is the man to whom the Lord will not impute sin." Because of our faith in Jesus Christ, God will not impute sin to us. That God will not impute our trespasses to us, is also described in Paul's second letter to the Corinthians:

19 To wit, that God was in Christ, reconciling the world unto himself, not imputing their trespasses unto them; and hath committed unto us the word of reconciliation. (2 Cor 5:19)

9 Cometh this blessedness then upon the circumcision only, or upon the uncircumcision also? for we say that faith was reckoned to Abraham for righteousness. 10 How was it then reckoned? when he was in circumcision, or in uncircumcision? Not in circumcision, but in uncircumcision. 11 And he received the sign of circumcision, a seal of the righteousness of the faith which he had yet being uncircumcised: that he might be the father of all them that believe, though they be not circumcised; that righteousness might be imputed unto them also: 12 And the father of circumcision to them who are not of the circumcision only, but who also walk in the steps of that faith of our father Abraham, which he had being yet uncircumcised. (Rom 4:9-12)

Next, Paul raises the question: Is this righteousness that God grants apart from our works only for the Jews (i.e. the circumcision)? He raises the question because only the Jews had circumcision, and Paul was writing to the believers in the city of Rome with its extensive pantheon of pagan Roman gods. Many of those believers, formerly pagan idol-worshipers, had never been circumcised. The answer to the question is given by pointing out that when Abraham was counted righteous, it was BEFORE he was circumcised, meaning that when it happened, he was just as uncircumcised as the Gentile believers in Rome! Paul thereby proves the uncircumcised Roman believers were counted by God just as righteous as their Jewish counterpart believers, for those Roman believers also had faith like Abraham's.

13 For the promise, that he should be the heir of the world, was not to Abraham, or to his seed, through the

law, but through the righteousness of faith. 14 For if they which are of the law be heirs, faith is made void, and the promise made of none effect: 15 Because the law worketh wrath: for where no law is, there is no transgression. 16 Therefore it is of faith, that it might be by grace; to the end the promise might be sure to all the seed; not to that only which is of the law, but to that also which is of the faith of Abraham; who is the father of us all (Rom 4:13-16)

Abraham, an old childless man, was given a promise by God that he would have an uncountable number of descendants.

4 And, behold, the word of the LORD came unto him, saying, This shall not be thine heir; but he that shall come forth out of thine own bowels shall be thine heir. 5 And he brought him forth abroad, and said, Look now toward heaven, and tell the stars, if thou be able to number them: and he said unto him, So shall thy seed be. 6 And he believed in the LORD; and he counted it to him for righteousness. (Gen 15:4-6)

The distinction of this promise is that Abraham would have many heirs, so many that he could not even count them anymore than he could count the stars in the sky. Through modern astronomy and our telescopes and computers, we now know our Sun and planets, our solar system, is part of the Milky Way galaxy. Estimates are our galaxy has anywhere between 200 billion to 400 billion stars. That is a vast number truly uncountable to someone standing underneath a clear night sky trying to count using just his human senses. That promise was not made under the Law of Moses, but long before Moses, and the promise was made on the basis of faith only.

Why is that important? Because any promised blessings of the Law were purely based on obedience to the Law. If Abraham's promise were dependent on people performing under the Law, then it would NEVER come about. Why? because of our sins would break the Law and nullify the behaviorally-based promise. As vs 15 above soberly says, "the law worketh wrath." Our sins do not get a reward, but instead earn us wrath! Thankfully, the promise was made, not on the basis of human works and performance where we could (and would) fail, but on the basis of simple faith in God.

Because it is not made under Law, we can't fail the conditions for the promise, and that makes the promise secure. God COULD have made the promise based on our performance, but He already knew how badly that would turn out. So, He made it as a matter and generosity of grace solely through faith.

So, you might ask, why are we going all over this promise made to Abraham, meaning, why is that important, and what's in it for me?

Paul answers that question, "to the end the promise might be sure to all the seed; not to that only which is of the law, but to that also which is of the faith of Abraham; who is the father of us all."

Abraham got that promise by grace through faith, so that you and I could also be included under it on the same basis of grace through faith.

Scripture describes our salvation this way:

8 For by grace are ye saved through faith; and that not of yourselves: it is the gift of God (Eph 2:8)

The righteousness we receive, is the righteousness received by Abraham, one obtained by grace though faith. As a forerunner of how a person receives righteousness apart from the Law, Abraham becomes in that sense a father to us all, Jew or Gentile.

17 (As it is written, I have made thee a father of many nations,) before him whom he believed, even God, who quickeneth the dead, and calleth those things which be not as though they were. 18 Who against hope believed in hope, that he might become the father of many nations; according to that which was spoken, So shall thy seed be. 19 And being not weak in faith, he considered not his own body now dead, when he was about an hundred years old, neither yet the deadness of Sara's womb: 20 He staggered not at the promise of God through unbelief; but was strong in faith, giving glory to God; 21 And being fully persuaded that, what he had promised, he was able also to perform. 22 And therefore it was imputed to him for righteousness. (Rom 4:17-22)

When God said, "I have made thee a father of many nations", it is interesting to note that God put it in the past tense. Even though Abraham was 100 years old and had not yet had a single child, yet from this we can learn that when God promises something, it is as good and certain to happen as if it had already happened. As the saying goes, "it's a done deal." God is the God who makes alive the dead, and calls things into being.

We can find tremendous consolation in this. If we have a need, and there seems to be no hope, no possible way to grant what we ask, and we yet pray, hoping against hope and trusting in God, even if nothing is in existence to solve the problem, God can call a solution INTO existence! Truly, nothing is impossible to God!

Here was Abraham's problem. As far as having a child was concerned, he was at 100 years old "dead", far and long past the years he could have fathered a child. His wife Sarah was 90, and she too was long past any hope of conceiving a child. Yet, because God promised, Abraham did not take into consideration the impossibility of his body's old age, but he hoped against hope, believing that because God promised it, it WOULD happen! Talk about an awesome faith! Would that we too would have faith like Abraham's!

God saw that faith, and imputed righteousness to Abraham. Now, we need to say something about the Greek word behind that word "imputed." I am at times amazed at how many people do not "get" what it means for God to have imputed righteousness to us. Going back to earlier in this chapter of Romans, we find:

3 For what saith the scripture? Abraham believed God, and it was counted unto him for righteousness. 4 Now to him that worketh is the reward not reckoned of grace, but of debt. 5 But to him that worketh not, but believeth on him that justifieth the ungodly, his faith is counted for righteousness. 6 Even as David also describeth the

blessedness of the man, unto whom God imputeth righteousness without works, 7 Saying, Blessed are they whose iniquities are forgiven, and whose sins are covered. 8 Blessed is the man to whom the Lord will not impute sin. (Romans 4:3-7)

In the above passage, we see the word "counted" twice, "reckoned" once, "impute" once, and "imputeth" once. Did you know that all these variations are the same word in Greek? It is Strong's G3049, λογίζομαι logizomai, which has a basic meaning of taking an inventory. Every merchant selling products takes an inventory in which the actual merchandise stock on hand is counted and verified. This helps keep the store shelves properly stocked.

You might ask, so why is the Apostle Paul using so many times in the above verses a word which speaks of counting up inventory?

Glad you asked.

The answer ties into eternal security (OSAS, Once-Saved-Always-Saved.)

You see, the basic problem of whether we make it to heaven to share eternity with God, or else get separated from Him in eternal torment in hell, has to do with sin and righteousness. Our problem is this: we are ALL sinners, so we all deserve hell. Just one "little" sin, makes us as guilty as if we had broken EVERY commandment of God.

10 For whosoever shall keep the whole law, and yet offend in one point, he is guilty of all. (James 2:10)

Moreover, God tells us that EVERY LAST ONE OF US HAS SINNED:

23 For all have sinned, and come short of the glory of God (Rom 3:23)

With such a standard, we can quickly see that there is no way any of us are capable of qualifying for entering heaven—we are just so sinful, we can't meet God's standard.

So, what's the deal with logizomai, you ask?

Just as a store takes an inventory, God does too. Let's illustrate what is at stake here.

Suppose there are two warehouses. Instead of keeping products for sale, they contain the amount of our sins and righteousness. The "sin" warehouse is filled with skid-loads of sins, the skids stacked to the ceiling and bulging at the warehouse's seams. The "righteousness" warehouse is empty, with maybe some dust bunnies in the corner.

Left to our own efforts, all we have to offer God is a warehouse loaded with our sins. God hates sin, so that means a total rejection for any hope of entering heaven. Yet, God knew that we were helpless and hopeless, so He chose, from before the world was created to solve the problem for us. Our sins deserve death, so God sent His Son Jesus to die death for us as a substitute for us.

Jesus got what He didn't deserve (death),

so that we could get what we don't deserve (life.)

Now, when we by faith place our hope of heaven in Jesus (not ourselves), God does some pretty impressive inventory work. (Oh, and the same word logizomai also gets used in the following verse, translated "imputing"):

19 To wit, that God was in Christ, reconciling the world unto himself, not imputing their trespasses unto them; and hath committed unto us the word of reconciliation. (2 Cor 5:19)

Did you catch that? God is NOT counting in our inventory the skid-loads of our sins. Imagine that He has a pen and pad of paper as He takes inventory. When we trust in Jesus Christ, God the Father checks the "sin" warehouse and writes His count of how many sins He is inventorying:

None. 0.

Let's look again at the above verse:
"… not imputing [logizomai] their trespasses unto them…"

"What!" cry you and I in amazement. "Doesn't He SEE all those sins I committed? Why is He marking the inventory of my sins as zero?"

Actually, what He is seeing is the blood Jesus shed on the cross for each and every one of those sins! The sacrifice of Jesus' death on the cross cancels the death penalty for those sins. He has atoned for our sins, and God the Father is fully satisfied with the deal. So, when we trust in Jesus, our sins are NOT counted anymore! As Romans says:

8 Blessed is the man to whom the Lord will not impute [logizomai] sin." (Romans 4:8)

But, it is not enough to cancel out the sins. God next visits our "righteousness" warehouse, which we saw earlier was empty of anything we could do, and instead of writing "None", the Father writes "FULL!"

"What!" cry you and I again! "Is He crazy?"

No, not at all. Because Jesus atoned for our sins, when we trust in Jesus, we are joined to Jesus spiritually. While we don't have (as the saying goes), "two dimes to rub together" as far as any righteousness of our own is concerned, God the Father credits us with the righteousness of JESUS HIMSELF! That's as good as it gets. There is no greater righteousness than that of God Himself, and THAT is what is credited [logizomai] to our account. Look at the below Scripture that speaks of how God credit us with His righteousness

21 But now the righteousness of God without the law is manifested, being witnessed by the law and the prophets; 22 Even the righteousness of God which is by faith of Jesus Christ unto all and upon all them that believe... (Rom 3:21-22a)

Do you see it? "the righteousness of God ... unto all and upon all them that believe." We are, because of "faith of Jesus Christ", clothed in the righteousness of God Himself!

This is so important to wrap our minds around it. Our

standing before God is that of perfectly righteous people. Not righteous because of what we do – or don't do – but because of faith in Jesus.

So, when someone tells you that you can lose your salvation (i.e. go to Hell), we surely need to ask on what basis are they determining their righteousness before God? If they are depending on ANYTHING other than faith in Jesus, then they are not understanding the true gospel that saves.

16 For I am not ashamed of the gospel of Christ: for it is the power of God unto salvation to every one that believeth; to the Jew first, and also to the Greek. 17 For therein is the righteousness of God revealed from faith to faith: as it is written, The just shall live by faith. (Romans 1:16-17)

Notice that salvation is "to every one that believeth", not "every one that behaveth."

It is by our faith, not our works; our belief, not our behavior. Why? Because we CAN'T behave as we should! We are sinners! That's the whole point of why we need a Savior! We are not "good enough", and never will be by our efforts for as long as we live out these mortal lives. Once God resurrects us, then we'll live correctly, but not until then.

But, notice this: Jesus IS "good enough". It is His merit that gets us into Heaven. His righteousness gets credited [logizomai] to our account because of our faith in Him.

So, those who believe you can lose your salvation, tell me how it is that someone counted [logizomai] as being as righteous as God Himself, can somehow "miss the boat" and not make it to heaven's shores?

Salvation truly is of the Lord, and not by ANYTHING we can do, or fail to do. Our part is solely to trust in Jesus that He died for our sins according to the Scripture, was buried, and rose again the third day according to the Scriptures.

Once we trust in Christ, we stand before God in total, perfect righteousness. It is because our righteousness is not earned, but imputed, that we see why a saved person cannot lose their salvation. Righteousness is not the result of anything a person has done, or failed to do, but is assigned by God the Father to a person who places faith in Jesus Christ. Seeing his heart of faith, God "logizomai"s righteousness to him that very moment. Since God dwells in eternity, that decision lasts for all eternity. That's why OSAS is true.

23 Now it was not written for his sake alone, that it was imputed to him; 24 But for us also, to whom it shall be imputed, if we believe on him that raised up Jesus our Lord from the dead; 25 Who was delivered for our offences, and was raised again for our justification. (Rom 4:23-25)

We just saw the explanation of "logizomai". We can now understand why the Apostle Paul went into so much detail over the promise God gave Abraham. Because God imputed ("logizomai") righteousness to Abraham solely on the basis of his faith in God, apart from any works, apart from commandments, and apart from being circumcised, then like the believers in ancient Rome, we can also know that God will also impute ("logizomai") righteousness to us by our simply believing God's message of the gospel, that Christ died for our sins, was buried, and rose again from the dead. Jesus went to the cross for our offences, the sins we have done and the commandments we have broken, ALL of them! When He rose again, it was for our justification. Remember, to "justify" means to declare righteous.

If we are a believer in Jesus Christ, no matter how many sins we have committed, because of our faith in Jesus, God counts us and declares us RIGHTEOUS! Amen!

Chapter 5

1 Therefore being justified by faith, we have peace with God through our Lord Jesus Christ: 2 By whom also we have access by faith into this grace wherein we stand, and rejoice in hope of the glory of God. (Rom 5:1-2)

In chapter 4, we saw the detailing of the witness of the Law and the prophets. Abraham was the example used from the Law, and David was the example from the prophets (Psalm 22 was a prophecy about the crucifixion of Jesus). Chapter 5 starts with the word "Therefore". A humorous admonition about that word says, when you see a "therefore", look to the previous text to see what the "therefore" is there for. Put it another way, a "therefore" means "on the basis of what we just covered."

So Paul says, on the basis that we have established there is a justification by faith apart from the commandments of the Law, we have what? Answer: "peace with God." The means of having that peace? Answer: "through our Lord Jesus Christ." The Son of God has made propitiation for our sins, and God's wrath is now SATISFIED. There is nothing more that Divine holiness, justice, vengeance and wrath can demand of the believer in Jesus Christ.

God is satisfied that the punishment for our sins is complete and total. If we can put it in human terms, God can relax and smile. He has successfully saved us who believe in Jesus. The deed is done, the job is over. Victory! We have peace with God now. No more worrying if He is going to smite us, send us to Hell.

This awesome work of God to rescue us from our sins has been done solely at His own choice to pay the terrible price

Himself. He didn't have to do it. He chose to do it, as a matter of pure grace! Not only do we get initially saved by grace, our standing with God – our status – remains one of grace. We are saved by grace, and we stand continually righteous before God because of that same grace.

And it gets even better. We "rejoice in hope of the glory of God." Because of our faith in Jesus, we have confidence that we will one day stand in the very Presence of God in all His glory, and will indeed be very welcomed by Him to spend all eternity with Him. Can't you just see Him smile in delight?

3 And not only so, but we glory in tribulations also: knowing that tribulation worketh patience; 4 And patience, experience; and experience, hope: 5 And hope maketh not ashamed; because the love of God is shed abroad in our hearts by the Holy Ghost which is given unto us. (Rom 5:3-5)

With this expectation that it only gets better in the future, we can face the present day troubles we encounter. We can learn patience, to "hang in there" despite our troubles, because we know what our glorious future holds for us. As we learn patience, we can face the experiences of tomorrow. In going through those experiences, we become stable and steadfast because we know this world's troubles are not all there is. We can see God's faithfulness in being with us through those experiences, that He will not leave or forsake us. Through our experiences, we rely more and more on our hope in God for the future, a confident expectation of the good and glory that will ultimately happen, no matter what troubles happen to us here on earth.

That hope takes away any shame for any mischief the world may cause us to suffer because we have a wonderful future promised by God. Why? because the love of God is shed abroad in our hearts by the Holy Ghost which is given unto us.

The love of God is so vast and deep, it is beyond our comprehension. Here is a verse describing the love of Jesus for us:

19 And to know the love of Christ, which passeth knowledge, that ye might be filled with all the fulness of God. (Eph 3:19 KJV)

I like how the New Living Translation describes it:
19 May you experience the love of Christ, though it is too great to understand fully. Then you will be made complete with all the fullness of life and power that comes from God. (Eph 3:10 NLT)

Christ's love for us "passeth knowledge", or "is too great to understand fully." That is the love that is "shed abroad in our hearts by the Holy Ghost"! That means, God the Father loves us that much; Jesus the Son loves us that much; and the Holy Spirit loves us that much!

The faithfulness of that love is revealed in this verse:

5 … for he hath said, I will never leave thee, nor forsake thee." (Heb 13:5b)

Such is the love of God that He will NEVER leave us! He loves us so much, He will NEVER forsake us! He loves us so much, He sent Jesus to lay down His life for us! And Jesus willingly and gladly did exactly that!

With this understanding, read again the most well-known verse in the Bible:

16 For God so loved the world, that he gave his only begotten Son, that whosoever believeth in him should not perish, but have everlasting life. (John 3:16)

How great is God's love for us? It is greater than we can fully understand!

6 For when we were yet without strength, in due time Christ died for the ungodly. 7 For scarcely for a righteous man will one die: yet peradventure for a good man some would even dare to die. 8 But God commendeth his love toward us, in that, while we were yet sinners, Christ died for us. (Rom 5:6-8)

During His time on earth, Jesus spoke of how we were without strength in terms of health and a doctor:

17 When Jesus heard it, he saith unto them, They that are whole have no need of the physician, but they that are sick: I came not to call the righteous, but sinners to repentance. (Mark 2:17)

Another way of saying "without strength" is "helpless":

6 For while we were still helpless, at the right time Christ died for the ungodly. (Rom 5:6 NASB)

Jesus is called the Great Physician. While He certainly healed many with physical illness, His greatest concern was for our spiritual illness, meaning that we were helpless sinners. He didn't die for "healthy" people. He died for "ungodly" people.

9 Much more then, being now justified by his blood, we shall be saved from wrath through him. 10 For if, when we were enemies, we were reconciled to God by the death

of his Son, much more, being reconciled, we shall be saved by his life. 11 And not only so, but we also joy in God through our Lord Jesus Christ, by whom we have now received the atonement. (Rom 5:9-11)

Paul points out results from the incredible favor God shows us. We are justified, that is, declared righteous, when we trust that Jesus shed His blood and died on the cross for us. The justification we have from God through our faith means God's wrath will not ever come upon us. Ever. Think of it. Because of our sins, we were rebels – enemies – of God. There is an expression people use: "Don't take it personally." The reverse is true for God. Our sins are not merely violations of His laws. God takes sin very "personally," as our sins are acts of treason against His very person. Put another way, our sins mean we reject Him, personally. The commandments are not merely arbitrary laws He put into effect, but are expressions of His own righteous being, His very Person.

Yet, through the cross, we have been reconciled. Things have been set right between us. The fury of God's anger and wrath have been satisfied. The personal insult of our sins against Him has been forgiven. Now that we have been reconciled, we are saved from that very wrath. God wants us to be His agents, His ambassadors, to let others know how they too can be reconciled.

20 Now then we are ambassadors for Christ, as though God did beseech you by us: we pray you in Christ's stead, be ye reconciled to God. (2 Cor 5:20)

Being saved is more than merely having our sins forgiven. It does something else wonderful. Instead of our cringing in fear, waiting for His furious hand to come down and swat us, we experience, of all things, JOY! This comes from approaching God through Jesus and the perfect atonement that He made for us on the cross. As it said earlier in this chapter, "the love of God is shed abroad in our hearts by the Holy Ghost which is given unto us." The joy we get in this salvation experience is the wonderful reality of the love God has for us, a love so amazing, and so deep and powerful, it "surpasseth knowledge." It is literally beyond our finite, mortal understanding. God's love for us is not merely how He acts toward us, but it is an expression of His very nature and being. It is as the Apostle John wrote, "God is love" (1 John 4:8, 16)

12 Wherefore, as by one man sin entered into the world, and death by sin; and so death passed upon all men, for that all have sinned: 13 (For until the law sin was in the world: but sin is not imputed when there is no law. 14 Nevertheless death reigned from Adam to Moses, even over them that had not sinned after the similitude of Adam's transgression, who is the figure of him that was to come. 15 But not as the offence, so also is the free gift. For if through the offence of one many be dead, much more the grace of God, and the gift by grace, which is by one man, Jesus Christ, hath abounded unto many. (Rom 5:12-15)

The word "wherefore" means "as a result of which." So, when the passage starts with "wherefore", it begins to describe the results of what was described beforehand, which was that we have atonement for our sins through Jesus. Paul now goes into finer details on exactly how this atonement covers, not just you or me, but all of us, and does this with a running comparison.

The sin of one man, Adam, affected not just himself, but the entire world. Because Adam sinned, you and I, his descendants, are subject to death. Why? Because we, too, have sinned.

While it is true that that breaking God's commandments evokes the death penalty, for a long time there were no commandments for the human race to break. From Adam to Moses, the only one commandment given to the human race was given in the Garden of Eden.

17 But of the tree of the knowledge of good and evil, thou shalt not eat of it: for in the day that thou eatest thereof thou shalt surely die. (Genesis 2:17)

But, with access to the Garden of Eden cut off, mankind no longer could break that commandment. That's why Paul wrote, "sin is not imputed when there is no law." God did not impute sin, infractions of the law, against us because there were no laws for us to break. Nevertheless, "death reigned from Adam to Moses," for we are all still sinners with a sin nature that WANTS to sin, and we, the human race, even though there was no commandments we could break, were still dying.

Now, Paul sets up a comparison between Adam and Christ.

By one man, Adam, we all get death from sin, even though we have not sinned the sin he did.

However, by a second man, Jesus (called by theologians the "second Adam"), we – that is, the entire human race – have available to us a free gift of atonement, a gift given to us by God by pure grace, undeserved, unmerited, unearned.

The first Adam got all of us into this mess. Our "second Adam" made the way for all of us to get out of the mess. Jesus did not make "a way", though, but Himself became "the way."

6 Jesus saith unto him, I am the way, the truth, and the life: no man cometh unto the Father, but by me. (John 14:6)

There are not many ways to God. There is only one way, and it is through Jesus Christ, and none other.

16 And not as it was by one that sinned, so is the gift: for the judgment was by one to condemnation, but the free gift is of many offences unto justification. 17 For if by one man's offence death reigned by one; much more they which receive abundance of grace and of the gift of righteousness shall reign in life by one, Jesus Christ.) 18 Therefore as by the offence of one judgment came upon all men to condemnation; even so by the righteousness of one the free gift came upon all men unto justification of life. 19 For as by one man's disobedience many were made sinners, so by the obedience of one shall many be made righteous. (Rom 5:16-19)

Another contrast occurs here. Adam's one sin resulted in condemnation upon the whole human race. All that for just one sin. Yet, we, the human race, are not guilty of just one sin, but of many sins!

Here is an illustration of this adapted from Evangelism Explosion (EE).

Suppose a real bad person (in our estimation) commits ten or more sins every hour. In contrast, suppose you or I, being "good" people, might only do only three sins per day, one bad word (cussing out someone who crossed us in traffic: "Why you dirty rat!"), one bad thought ("I'll show you a thing or two!"), or one bad action (get revenge by cutting off that other driver: "There, that will teach you not to mess with me!"). Other than that, we're practically what people would call a saint.

Yet, there are 365 days in our calendar year. At just 3 sins a day, we commit over 1,000 sins in a year! By the time we are adults, our sins amass into the tens of thousands of sins!

The free gift of atonement "is of many offences unto justification." Many offenses, indeed. Yet that same free gift grants us justification, and despite our tens of thousands of sins, it is by this free gift of God's grace that we are counted by God as RIGHTEOUS!

It boggles the mind that God can look upon us, who have committed an incredible number of tens of thousands of sins, and yet declare us righteous. Such is the power of the cross of Jesus Christ and the atonement He made there for us, making propitiation to satisfy God's wrath against our almost uncountable number of sins!

If we each were under the penalty of death because of Adam's sin, it is all the more amazing that with God's gift of righteousness through faith in Jesus Christ that we "shall reign in life". It is all because of Jesus!

Paul continues to make contrasts. Why the repetition? So that we finally "get it". He wants us to understand why we, though sinners, are counted righteous in God's eyes.

So, as Adam's one offense we all fell under judgment and were condemned to death, so it is that our second Adam's sacrifice made the free gift of righteousness available to all of us for us to have life.

As one man's disobedience, Adam's, made sinners of us all, so the obedience of one man, Jesus, our second Adam, we can all be made righteous.

20 Moreover the law entered, that the offence might abound. But where sin abounded, grace did much more abound: 21 That as sin hath reigned unto death, even so might grace reign through righteousness unto eternal life by Jesus Christ our Lord. (Rom 5:20-21)

Now, even as we know now that death reigned from Adam until Moses, even though there was only one commandment given to us, one which was no longer possible to break, yet with Moses there came 613 more commandments in the Law. With the entrance into world history of the Law of Moses, the number of offences, the actual breaking of God's commandments that could be charged as crimes against people, increased exponentially.

Yet, here in verse 20, we find an amazing proof of eternal security, also known as OSAS (once-saved-always-saved).

"But where sin abounded, grace did much more abound".

Look carefully at this text where it says sin "abounded." That means, grew to an overwhelming number, an abundance! When we look honestly at our sins in light of the three-sins-a-day illustration, we have not just a few sins, or maybe a pile of sins. No, we have a MOUNTAIN of sins!

The Greek word for "abound" in this passage is πλεονάζω pleonazō. It means, "to superabound."

But, when we come to God with a mountain of sins ("where sin abounded"), God gives us an even greater mountain of grace ("grace did much more abound").

The Greek word for "much more abound" is ὑπερπερισσεύω hyperperisseuō. It means, "to abound beyond measure, abound exceedingly."

No matter how many sins we have, when we come to God through faith in Jesus Christ, even with an exponentially increased superabundance of sins, God has an even greater abundance of grace, which abounds "beyond measure." We cannot out-sin God's grace! We are eternally secure from losing our salvation because of God's grace "beyond measure."

Chapter 6

1 What shall we say then? Shall we continue in sin, that grace may abound? (Rom 6:1)

I was leading a Bible study on this chapter, when it became clear to me that the secret of how to overcome temptation to sin is hidden in plain view. Almost every Christian fights with some sin or other. We fight, and much too often, we lose. Why is that?

The answer is surprisingly simple: We try overcoming sin the wrong way. Happily, both the wrong way and the right way are revealed to us in Romans 6. Once it becomes clear how to fight sin the right way, many of our sin battles will find victory at the end instead of defeat.

Now, every Christian knows Jesus died for our sin on the cross, was buried for three days, and rose from the dead in a bodily resurrection. We also know that when we trust in Him by faith, God saves us by His grace. Grace is defined as an undeserved gift. It's also been illustrated in an acrostic:

G – God's
R – Riches
A – At
C – Christ's
E – Expense

As we grow in our knowledge of God's word, we learn that no amount of good works can save us. The human tendency to "work" our way into Heaven is very common, indeed, universal. We instinctively try to do good works by obeying God's Law, which includes the Ten Commandments, but Scripture tells us no one can be saved by the works of the law. (Galatians 2:16) We are saved by grace, not law.

All too often, though, what happens once we are already saved is that we try to overcome the temptation to sin by switching back to the works of the law. That is the wrong way mentioned earlier. Let's see the wrong way—and the right way—explained and taught.

In the previous chapter 5, we saw that once we are saved, we are always and forever saved. You know someone understands the implications of God's grace that saves us— and keeps us saved—when they ask something like, "You mean, I can go out and do all sorts of sins, and still go to Heaven?"

While that question shows a grasp of the implications of grace, the conclusion reached is really not the correct conclusion we should draw, as we shall see in this study of Romans 6. Starting at verse 1, we find Paul anticipating someone's jumping to that conclusion by asking the question, "Shall we continue in sin, that grace may abound?"

This question comes from implications derived from Paul's statement we saw last chapter:

20 ...But where sin abounded, grace did much more abound: (Romans 5:20b)
How does Paul respond?

2 God forbid. How shall we, that are dead to sin, live any longer therein? (Rom 6:2)

The answer given by Divine inspiration of the Holy Spirit through Paul is sharp: "God forbid."

We saw last chapter that even if we have a mountain of sins to give God, He has an even bigger mountain of Grace to cover it. When that realization sinks in and we understand that we cannot out-sin God's grace, that's when the implications of grace sink in as well. Once saved, ALWAYS saved! God's grace covers it ALL! So, when we finally grasp the truth "But where sin abounded, grace did much more abound", in true human fashion we jump to the wrong conclusion, "Well, then I can just go out and sin all I want because grace will just increase to cover me." This is what Paul is expressing in Romans 6:1, What shall we say then? Shall we continue in sin, that grace may abound?

He then goes on to say why that idea is not right.

3 Know ye not, that so many of us as were baptized into Jesus Christ were baptized into his death? 4 Therefore we are buried with him by baptism into death: that like as Christ was raised up from the dead by the glory of the Father, even so we also should walk in newness of life. (Rom 6:3-4)

Paul says we "died to sin." How is this possible? What does he mean? When I trusted Christ, I didn't die, did I? I'm still breathing, my heart is still beating, so I'm still alive, right? It should be obvious that Paul is not talking about physical matters, but spiritual ones. He is using physical terms we can see to explain spiritual ones we can't see. With a spiritual focus, then, let's follow Paul's line of reasoning. What he means by it, we shall see become clearer as Romans 6 goes on. He teaches us that we have "died to sin" in a spiritual sense, and then raises the question, "(how shall we) still live in it?"

In human terms, death is the ultimate separator. There's no going back. It is final to humans, but not to God "who gives life to the dead." (Romans 4:17b)

Baptism is celebrated throughout the world by Christians. Inwardly, we have been baptized by the Holy Spirit (Luke 3:16; Acts 2:3-4; Ephesians 1:13-14). Outwardly, we practice water baptism. Water baptism does not save us, nor add anything to our salvation (1 Corinthians 1:14-17). What water baptism does is to illustrate outwardly a spiritual reality that happened inwardly in a believer's life. When someone is water baptized, they are lowered fully under the water, then after a moment are lifted back up to the air and sunshine again. When the believer is lowered beneath the water, symbolically it paints a picture of a believer's death and burial to our old sinful life. When lifted back up out of the water, it symbolizes resurrection to new life.

So when verse 3 says "we have been baptized into Christ Jesus," it is saying that we are identified with Jesus Christ and joined to Him (1 Corinthians 6:17). When He goes, we go. Where we go, He goes (1 Corinthians 6:15-16). By virtue of being baptized into Christ Jesus by our faith, we are counted as having died to sin and buried when Jesus died and was buried, and we are counted as having arisen to new spiritual life when He rose from the dead.

Christianity isn't about rules and regulations. It isn't even about just knowing things about Jesus. It's rather about being joined to Him spiritually for the long haul, meaning forever. Where He goes, we go. We are inseparably joined to Him as members of His body (1 Corinthians 12:27).

Now that Jesus has risen from the dead in a newness of eternal life, so Scripture is teaching us that we, too, now are alive from the dead and walk in newness of life:

5 For if we have been planted together in the likeness of his death, we shall be also in the likeness of his resurrection: 6 Knowing this, that our old man is crucified with him, that the body of sin might be destroyed, that henceforth we should not serve sin. 7 For he that is dead is freed from sin. (Rom 6:5-7)

We Christians live in a dual existence. In the spiritual realm, we are children of God (John 1:12; Romans 8:4; Ephesians 5:1-2; 1 Peter 1:23; 1 John 3:1-3). Yet, in the physical realm, we each yet live in a physical body of flesh and blood which carries in it sinful impulses to "do its own thing," which means, to rebel against God and His law, indeed, against ANY law, whether God's or Man's. (Hint: When you see a beautiful lawn of lush green grass inviting you to swish your feet through it, but with a sign that says STAY OFF THE GRASS, what's your first impulse?)

This begins to get to the heart of why we sin still, even after believing in Jesus Christ and being saved forever. There are two dynamics working in us, one tugging at us to do good, and the other tugging at us to do evil (Galatians 5:17). Now we've seen WHY we sin. In Romans 6, Paul teaches us the foundation for WHAT we can do about it, meaning, how to overcome sin the right way. In verse 7, he writes, "For he that is dead is freed from sin." The word "freed" carries with it the idea of liberation and escape from slavery and tyranny. We must understand that before we believed in Christ, we were slaves of sin. We had no choice but to follow its directives, impulses and urges. Now, in Christ, we are set free. (More on this later.)

8 Now if we be dead with Christ, we believe that we shall also live with him: 9 Knowing that Christ being raised from the dead dieth no more; death hath no more dominion over him. 10 For in that he died, he died unto sin once: but in that he liveth, he liveth unto God. (Rom 6:8-10)

The above passage says, "If we be dead with Christ." If we are believers, then this is spiritually true of us. Moreover, we have the knowledge that we, too, will live with Him. This isn't only a statement that our bodies will one day be resurrected as Christ's was on that Resurrection Sunday (aka Easter.) It is also a statement of the spiritual reality that we Christians, being born-again children of God, have a new spiritual life living in us today that we did not possess before believing in Jesus.

Just as Jesus died to our sin (and through our being joined to Him, we have, too), now He lives to God, and we do, too. With this foundation laid, Paul now instructs us how to rightly overcome temptations to sin:

11 Likewise reckon ye also yourselves to be dead indeed

unto sin, but alive unto God through Jesus Christ our Lord. (Rom 6:11)

Let's review why this is truly the way to rightly overcome sin. In verse 6, we find, "knowing this, that our old self was crucified with Him..." Crucifixion is fatal. It is vitally important that we know this, and on the basis of it, consider ourselves "dead to sin."

Let me illustrate. Suppose we are at a wake mourning over a friend who died. This friend was, to be honest, very overweight. He loved hot fudge sundaes, and could not resist the impulse to eat that ice cream creation at every possible opportunity. Suppose we bring an extra-large hot fudge sundae to the open coffin, wave it suggestively before his face, and say, "Mmmm, look at what I have here, my friend, a double-sized hot fudge sundae." Believers, let's lock that image in our minds. Our friend is dead to hot fudge sundaes. They can no longer entice him. They have no more power over him.

So it is, as a spiritual reality, that we are to consider ourselves as being dead to sins. When a temptation to any sin comes along, we are not to go back and forth struggling and wavering over whether or not to do it. That is entirely irrelevant. Does that our friend in the coffin struggle over whether or not to eat that hot fudge sundae? No! Of course not! There is no consideration of it at all. He is DEAD to it! Likewise concerning a temptation to sin, we are to simply reckon in our hearts, "I am dead to this."

But, this is only half the picture. The verse doesn't stop at being "dead to sin," but tells us we are also to consider ourselves, "alive to God in Christ Jesus." So, when temptation to sin comes along, we need to reckon within ourselves, "I am dead to this, but I am alive to God in Christ Jesus."

Paul also wrote of this in his letter to the Colossians:
1 If ye then be risen with Christ, seek those things which are above, where Christ sitteth on the right hand of God. 2 Set your affection on things above, not on things on the earth. 3 For ye are dead, and your life is hid with Christ in God. 4 When Christ, who is our life, shall appear, then shall ye also appear with him in glory. 5 Mortify therefore your members which are upon the earth; fornication, uncleanness, inordinate affection, evil concupiscence, and covetousness, which is idolatry: 6 For which things' sake the wrath of God cometh on the children of disobedience: 7 In the which ye also walked some time, when ye lived in them. 8 But now ye also put off all these; anger, wrath, malice, blasphemy, filthy communication out of your mouth. (Col 3:1-8)
To "mortify" (vs 5) is an old English word meaning "put to death." We are to count ourselves as dead to sins, but alive to God by faith in Jesus Christ, who does not merely have our life, but rather He is our life!

12 Let not sin therefore reign in your mortal body, that ye should obey it in the lusts thereof. 13 Neither yield ye your members as instruments of unrighteousness unto sin: but yield yourselves unto God, as those that are alive from the dead, and your members as instruments of righteousness unto God. (Rom 6:12-13)

For anyone who has felt trapped and helpless in a sin habit or addiction, the above verses may seem shocking or incredible. Verse 12 says, "let not sin therefore reign." The word "let" speaks of permission, as in allowing it to happen. Yes, that's right. If you are feeling trapped in a sin habit or addiction, you are that way because you "let" it happen. The GOOD NEWS is that it doesn't have to hold you any longer. Look at verse 13: "Neither yield ye." It's saying, don't yield to it, or allow it any more. If you're caught in a habit or addiction, stay with this just a bit longer. Trust Jesus! You can be free!

We are instructed, "Neither yield ye." This means we aren't helpless—we have a choice, and knowing we have a choice should reignite a flame of hope instead of despair. Then we're told, "Neither yield ye your members as instruments of unrighteousness unto sin". The idea here is voluntarily surrendering our bodies to their sinful impulses. Picture two enemy soldiers. One has a rifle with a bayonet. That soldier voluntarily hands his weapon to the enemy, who promptly takes it and stabs the first with his own bayonet.

This picture is what is meant by "yield ye your members as instruments of unrighteousness unto sin." When we surrender our bodies to sinful impulses, we're equipping sin with the tools to do us harm. So, Paul tells us to do instead is, "but yield yourselves unto God, as those that are alive from the dead, and your members as instruments of righteousness unto God."

We died to sin, and (in our illustration) to hot fudge sundaes. We are now rather alive to God. Since we are dead to sin, no sin habit or addiction can truly hold us in its power, unless we allow it by surrendering ourselves to it. We only have two choices: surrender to sin, or surrender to

God. Ask yourself this, "Which choice is better?"

14 For sin shall not have dominion over you: for ye are not under the law, but under grace. (Rom 6:14)

If you have been following this study so far, the question ought to arise in your mind, "Why is Paul bringing up being 'under the law?'" Indeed, since Paul has been teaching us that we are dead to sin, then why does he bring up the law?

Instead of inquiring into the law, should we not be asking the question, "How is it that a Christian, who has died to sin and is alive to God, can be seemingly trapped in a particular sin habit or addiction?" Why has Paul's line of reasoning gone to the law? The answer to both questions is the same.

Paul wrote to the Corinthians:

56 The sting of death is sin, and the power of sin is the law. (1 Corinthians 15:56)

The power of sin is the law. Think about that for a moment. The power ... of sin ... is the law. I said earlier that there are two dynamics working in us. One of them is called "the flesh" which wants to rebel against any law, whether God's Law (like the Ten Commandments) or Man's law. A sober truth about our natures and the law, is that law stirs up rebellion in our hearts (Romans 7:5), and actually strengthens our temptations to entice us to give into sin. "The power of sin is the law."

Returning to Romans 6, where Paul is teaching us how to overcome sin, we now know the reason Paul is telling us in

Romans 6:14b, "... for ye are not under the law, but under grace."

The "wrong way" is try to fight temptation with law-keeping.

Let me illustrate. Suppose I sin. I am grieved (under the Holy Spirit's conviction) that I did it. So I repent, and promise I won't do it again. Sounds normal and natural, right? But it's the wrong way to overcome sin. The moment I make a promise "I won't do it again," I've put myself under a law, namely, "I shalt not do it again."

The power of sin is the law. Now, having put myself under a law not to do it again, the next time temptation comes along, it's actually harder to resist than it was before, because putting myself under a law has given power to the sin. So, I give in the next time, and not only do I feel guilty for having done it, but also I feel bad that I broke my promise. So, I promise ever harder, "I really won't do it again." However, this just puts me under law even further. The power of sin is the law. When that temptation comes along again, I fall for it even easier than the last time. So, I put myself under an even harsher law than before, "I absolutely won't do it again."

On and on the cycle goes, repenting and putting myself more and more under law by my ever-stronger promises. The outcome is that eventually I run out of willpower and hope. I despair and cry out, "I am such a loser! I keep doing the same sin! I'm hopeless! I keep breaking my word and disappointing God!" Then I go on to despair of how God could ever love someone as deplorable and despicable as me.

That cycle is described later in Scripture in Romans 7:15-23 (which we will cover in the next chapter). That being said, notice the despairing cry at the cycle's conclusion:

24 Wretched man that I am! Who will set me free from the body of this death? (Romans 7:24)

The answer, happily, is given immediately:

25 Thanks be to God through Jesus Christ our Lord! (Romans 7: 25a)

God sets us free by His grace through our faith in Jesus Christ.

Paul also described this idea of trying to please God by the efforts of our flesh and law-keeping in his writing to the Galatians:

1 You foolish Galatians, who has bewitched you, before whose eyes Jesus Christ was publicly portrayed as crucified? 2 This is the only thing I want to find out from you: did you receive the Spirit by the works of the Law, or by hearing with faith? 3 Are you so foolish? Having begun by the Spirit, are you now being perfected by the flesh? (Galatians 3:1-3)

We are NOT "being perfected by the flesh" by "the works of the law." We are being perfected by God's grace through faith in Jesus Christ!

So, coming back to Romans 6:14b, we again read, "for ye are not under the law, but under grace." Paul is teaching in Romans 6 the right way to overcome sin. When faced with temptation, there is a wrong way to respond, and a right way to respond. The wrong way is to respond with law: "I won't do that. I must not do that. It's wrong." This is a "law" response. Remember, "the power of sin is the law." Paul has already taught us, "ye are not under the law, but under grace."

Now, contrast this with the right way to respond to temptation: "I am dead to this sin, but alive to God through Jesus Christ."

This is a "grace" response. We don't have to submit to and obey laws to please God! Rather, we submit to God's grace, and THAT pleases God!

15 What then? shall we sin, because we are not under the law, but under grace? God forbid. (Rom 6:15)

Now, still anticipating the implications of grace and how someone could still jump to the wrong conclusion, Paul continues to write.

It seems we humans are tenaciously and almost incurably "religious," in that we want to please God with our works in order to be acceptable to Him. When our religious nature gets confronted and shattered by grace, we jump from one extreme to the other, FROM stern repression of sinful impulses through religion TO rampant indulgence in those sinful impulses when we realize the penalty has already been paid for us by God's grace.

How foolish we are!

16 Know ye not, that to whom ye yield yourselves servants to obey, his servants ye are to whom ye obey; whether of sin unto death, or of obedience unto righteousness? (Rom 6:16)

Having revealed our freedom through grace by faith in Jesus, Paul again shows why turning to rampant sin is a bad idea. We humans were created to serve. Sin is a terrible taskmaster, driving us to do despicable and hateful things, and herds us along toward death.

In contrast, Jesus said, "Come to me, all who are weary and heavy laden, and I will give you rest. Take My yoke upon you and learn from Me, for I am gentle and humble in heart, and you will find rest for your souls. For My yoke is easy and My burden is light." (Matthew 11:28-30)

Singer Bob Dylan, after his conversion to Jesus Christ, did a song in which he sang, "You got to serve somebody. It may be the devil or it may be the Lord, but you got to serve somebody."

We were created to serve, so which will we choose: sin, that we may die; or Jesus, that we may live?

17 But God be thanked, that ye were the servants of sin, but ye have obeyed from the heart that form of doctrine which was delivered you. 18 Being then made free from sin, ye became the servants of righteousness. 19 I speak after the manner of men because of the infirmity of your

flesh: for as ye have yielded your members servants to uncleanness and to iniquity unto iniquity; even so now yield your members servants to righteousness unto holiness. 20 For when ye were the servants of sin, ye were free from righteousness. (Rom 6:17-20)

The wrong way to live is in verse 19a. As we have presented ourselves to impurity and lawlessness by giving ourselves over to those things, it resulted "to iniquity unto iniquity", meaning, "in further lawlessness." This means that giving in to sin just makes it easier to give in the next time, and the next, and the next, and so on. This is where sin habits and addictions find their beginning.

The right way to live is in verse 19b, "So now present your members as slaves to righteousness." Our slavery to sin and its power has been broken by Jesus Christ! Now, as believers, we are able to give in to righteous deeds, "resulting in sanctification."

Now, I'm going to back up a bit to recap the wrong way and the right way to overcome sin.

Verse 11: "Likewise reckon ye also yourselves to be dead indeed unto sin, but alive unto God through Jesus Christ our Lord."

Verse 12: "Let not sin therefore reign in your mortal body, that ye should obey it in the lusts thereof."

Verse 14: "For sin shall not have dominion over you: for ye are not under the law, but under grace."

If we respond to temptation in a "grace" way, then sin will NOT reign, nor be master over us. However, if we respond in a "law" way, then the reverse will be true -- sin WILL reign in our mortal bodies, and it WILL be master over us.

In light of this, fellow believers, if we have a sin habit or addiction the power of which we can't break, what does that say about which way we have been responding to temptation: the "grace" way or the "law" way? Scripture testifies, "The power of sin is the law." (1 Corinthians 15:56b)

If sin has power in our lives, then it becomes clear that we have been responding in a "law" way, does it not? If we want to be free, we need to go back to grace. For the believer, there's no time like now to be set free, for there is no amount or excess of sin that God hasn't already covered in overflowing grace through our faith in Jesus shedding His blood and dying for us on the cross to pay the penalty for our sins!

Finally, Paul concludes Romans 6:

21 What fruit had ye then in those things whereof ye are now ashamed? for the end of those things is death. 22 But now being made free from sin, and become servants to God, ye have your fruit unto holiness, and the end everlasting life. 23 For the wages of sin is death; but the gift of God is eternal life through Jesus Christ our Lord. (Rom 6:21-23)

If we have a sin habit or addiction, are we not ashamed of it? Realistically, there's no benefit to such, only death. Yet, we can now take heart! We have been "freed from sin" and "enslaved to God." For many people, slavery invokes a picture of shame and unpleasantness, but serving God is shockingly different, for it is life-giving and joyful. In Christ Jesus, we ... are ...FREE! That sin habit or addiction is NO match for the awesome power and grace of God. To be free, take to heart verse 13, "and do not go on presenting the members of your body as instruments of unrighteousness; but present yourselves to God as those alive from the dead, and your members as instruments of righteousness to God."

For someone with an addiction, whether to pornography, drugs or alcohol, there is a physical component involved as well as a spiritual one. Where a physical addiction is involved, such as alcohol or drugs, the Lord may direct us to seek medical help. Yet, even these addictions are no match for God's grace and our freedom in Christ Jesus. For someone addicted, there is going to have to be some gut-honest humbling of self, confessing it and acknowledging that we gave ourselves over to it; yet, this is exactly what God wants us to do. As the above Scripture says, do not go on presenting the members of your body (to sin) ... but present yourselves to God (by grace, not law) as those dead to sin and alive to God through Jesus Christ.

We have each of us been freed from sin. Now it's time to live free in that truth. Learn to respond to each day's temptations in a "grace" way, and present the members of your body to God for righteousness, and you will exult in an astonishing freedom you'd otherwise given up all hope of ever experiencing. Consider yourself dead to sin but alive to God through Christ Jesus! Be free!

Chapter 7

1 Know ye not, brethren, (for I speak to them that know the law,) how that the law hath dominion over a man as long as he liveth? (Rom 7:1)

As Paul writes to the Romans, he knows that even as the Israelites had the Law of Moses, the Romans had their own laws. The Romans were a people who "know the law." There were severe penalties for anyone who broke Caesar's laws. However, no matter how severe, Laws can only have dominion over someone only as long as they are alive. Death nullifies the demands of any law, Mosaic or Roman.

2 For the woman which hath an husband is bound by the law to her husband so long as he liveth; but if the husband be dead, she is loosed from the law of her husband. 3 So then if, while her husband liveth, she be married to another man, she shall be called an adulteress: but if her husband be dead, she is free from that law; so that she is no adulteress, though she be married to another man. (Rom 7:2-3)

As an object lesson, Paul uses the most universal law known to mankind, the law of marriage. The phrase "until death do us part" is a very common part of the marriage vows anywhere in the world. A person stays with their spouse for as long as they both shall live, and if they stray to another person, it is adultery. But the spouse dies, then they are free to remarry and it is not adultery.

4 Wherefore, my brethren, ye also are become dead to the law by the body of Christ; that ye should be married

**to another, even to him who is raised from the dead, that
we should bring forth fruit unto God. (Rom 7:4)**

Paul then applies the marriage law to the Church. The
Church, symbolized as the wife married to the Law, has died
(which we covered in last chapter). Because of that death,
the "marriage" of people to the Law is now null and void. It
has no power anymore over people who have died to it, just
as death annuls a marriage when one of the spouses dies. As
last chapter said, "Likewise reckon ye also yourselves to be
dead indeed unto sin, but alive unto God through Jesus
Christ our Lord." Now that we who believe are dead to sin
but raised to life in Christ, we can be seen as the spouse who
remarries because the former spouse has died. We are now
spiritually and legally joined to Christ.
17 But he that is joined unto the Lord is one spirit. (12 Cor
6:17)

As a result of this "remarriage", where we were dead to sin
but alive to God through Christ Jesus. We now seek to bring
forth fruit ("good works") to God.

10 For we are His workmanship, created in Christ Jesus for
good works, which God prepared beforehand so that we
would walk in them. (Eph 2:10)

**5 For when we were in the flesh, the motions of sins,
which were by the law, did work in our members to
bring forth fruit unto death. (Rom 7:5)**

While in the flesh (not saved), our sinful passions were
aroused by the Law. Remember from Romans chapter 6, we
saw the wrong way to overcome sin and its temptations by

trying to defeat them by Law-keeping? We saw 1 Cor 15:56 at work: "the power of sin is the law." The Law actually stirs up rebellion in our hearts. Instead of giving life as Grace does, the Law brings death! The law does not applaud us for doing Good, but it only condemns us for doing Evil.

6 But now we are delivered from the law, that being dead wherein we were held; that we should serve in newness of spirit, and not in the oldness of the letter. (Rom 7:6)

As Paul shows us from the illustration of death freeing the remaining spouse from the marriage bond, we are told "now we are delivered from the law." Through Christ we have died to our old "marriage partner", the Law, and are released from it. Freed from our old "marriage partner", we are now free to be "married" to our new "spouse", Christ. We don't try living in the past, the "oldness of the letter", but now live in the newness of the spiritual life we have through the indwelling Holy Spirit.

An error so many people make is the idea that since I am saved, then I can go out and sin all I want. Yet, Jesus did not save us to go out and serve sin. He saved us to live in the holiness of the new spiritual life He has given us.

7 What shall we say then? Is the law sin? God forbid. Nay, I had not known sin, but by the law: for I had not known lust, except the law had said, Thou shalt not covet. (Rom 7:7)

Paul repeats that we are not to go out and sin all we want. Instead, we are free from Law. Why is that important?

Because "the power of sin is the law" (1 Cor 15:56). As long as we are trying to defeat temptation through being under Law, we are fighting a losing battle against sin empowered by the Law. The Law is not itself sin, but rather it gives us an unchanging definition of what sin is. Because of the "thou shalt nots" of the Law, we know those things forbidden are sin.

Because of the tie-in of the Law and how it gives power to sin, some might be confused about the role of the Law, so Paul asks, "What shall we say then? Is the law sin?" The answer is a sharp, No! God forbid!

8 But sin, taking occasion by the commandment, wrought in me all manner of concupiscence. For without the law sin was dead. (Rom 7:8)

The problem in us is that when we are told, don't covet, our sinful impulses do the opposite and so we covet. Sin uses the commandment to jump into action.

Consider the following contrast:
Apart from the law, sin is dead (Rom 7;8)
The power of sin is the law (1 Cor 15:56)

The presence of Law in our lives empowers sin, but the lack of Law deadens it. This then makes more sense of what Paul wrote in Romans chapter 6 when he said, "For sin shall not have dominion over you: for ye are not under the law, but under grace." Law gives dominion to sin in our lives; grace takes away that dominion. As we saw in last chapter, operating under Law is trying to overcome sin the wrong way. We CAN'T be victorious using Law against temptation. Success is by Grace, not Law.

9 For I was alive without the law once: but when the commandment came, sin revived, and I died. 10 And the commandment, which was ordained to life, I found to be unto death. 11 For sin, taking occasion by the commandment, deceived me, and by it slew me. (Rom 7:9-11)

Scholars have debated whether Paul next to speaking of his life as a man before he knew Jesus as his Savior, or after as a saved man. I think the answer is neither, or perhaps I really should say, both. What follows is more of an illustration of the practical outworking of the relationship between Law and sin.

He says, "I was alive without the law." Obviously Paul is not speaking of life and death in a physical sense, for his heart did not stop beating and his lungs did not stop breathing when he wrote "and I died." Moreover, he was not spiritually alive at one point, and then died spiritually. Why do I say that? Because all of us were born with sin natures that made us spiritually dead before we took our first breath at physical birth. Rather he is speaking of life and death by way of illustration to explain the futility of trying to overcome sin by keeping the commandments of the Law. He vindicates God's Law by showing the problem is not with God's Law, but with us. When a commandment came from God, it stirred up rebellion in our sinful hearts. God's Law is life itself *IF* we are righteous, but it is Death if we are unrighteous.

Interesting, isn't it, that Paul says of sin that it "deceived me." When a temptation gets the better of us, it deceives us into thinking that what the temptation if offering is too valuable and desirable to miss or pass up. Being deceived by that allure, we give in to temptation and sin.

Thus the truth is revealed. The "too-good-to-be-true" promise of temptation turns out to be exactly that: not true. Though sin promises fulfilment and life, it delivers emptiness and death. Sin brings misery, not joy. Yet, we all too often give in, and reap dreadful consequences.

Remember that when the Bible tells us that what we sow, that we also reap, there are three phases to that:
1) We reap WHAT we sow
2) We reap LATER than we sow
3) We reap MORE than we sow.

When we sin, we sow the wind, but reap the whirlwind (Hosea 8:7). What is a whirlwind? It is a strong wind that whirls round and round. In other words, a whirlwind is what we call a twister, or tornado, a destructive whirling wind that tears up trees and destroys houses and lives.

12 Wherefore the law is holy, and the commandment holy, and just, and good. 13 Was then that which is good made death unto me? God forbid. But sin, that it might appear sin, working death in me by that which is good; that sin by the commandment might become exceeding sinful. (Rom 7:12-13)

The Law is vindicated, being holy, just and good. Yet note that the Law itself didn't become death for us. Let the blame be placed where it belong: sin is the real culprit. Law provokes the sin within us to rise up and be seen for what it really is. It is like taking a sharp pointed stick and poking a sleeping lion with it. The commandments pull away the mask of the hideous face of sin to show us how bad sin really is!

14 For we know that the law is spiritual: but I am carnal, sold under sin. (Rom 7:14)

We who are saved live in two worlds at the same time, one foot in the physical world and one foot in the spiritual world. In the spiritual realm, the Law, we have seen, is holy, just and good. Yet our bodies in the physical world, called "flesh", are steeped in sin. Our flesh is in bondage, slavery, to sin. In our flesh, we CANNOT obey God's Law.

15 For that which I do I allow not: for what I would, that do I not; but what I hate, that do I. 16 If then I do that which I would not, I consent unto the law that it is good. (Rom 7:15-16)

We are caught in a crossfire of a war between the spiritual, the Spirit, and the physical, the flesh.

17 For the flesh lusteth against the Spirit, and the Spirit against the flesh: and these are contrary the one to the other: so that ye cannot do the things that ye would. (Gal 5:17)

In our spirit, we would like to do the right thing, but the impulse to sin fights against that, urging us to do the wrong thing. Jesus aid, "The spirit truly is ready, but the flesh is weak" (Mark 14:38b).

Paul goes on to tell us that when in our hearts we want to do the right thing, it is us confessing the Law is good and right, because we agreeing with it. That is why we want to obey the Ten Commandments.

17 Now then it is no more I that do it, but sin that dwelleth in me. 18 For I know that in me (that is, in my flesh,) dwelleth no good thing: for to will is present with me; but how to perform that which is good I find not. (Rom 7:17-18)

So, if the Law is good, and we want to obey it, where is the problem that causes us to do what we hate? The answer is simple: sins dwells in our flesh.

19 For the good that I would I do not: but the evil which Iould not, that I do. 20 Now if I do that I would not, it is no more I that do it, but sin that dwelleth in me. 21 I find then a law, that, when I would do good, evil is present with me. 22 For I delight in the law of God after the inward man: 23 But I see another law in my members, warring against the law of my mind, and bringing me into captivity to the law of sin which is in my members. (Rom 7:19-23)

Look at Paul's description of the frustrating inability to do good. When we want to do good, but end up doing the wrong we don't want, it shows us that there is a principle that evil is in us, specifically, in our flesh.

In our hearts, despite that we agree with God's Law, we yet see evil operating in us despite our best good intentions, evil that does NOT agree with God's Law, but rebels against it.

We saw earlier that "the power of sin is the Law." The lawlessness in us is offended by the Law, and rises up to oppose it. The stronger the Law, the stronger the rebellion in our hearts.

What a terrible fight, the law of evil in our flesh, versus the Law of God in our hearts!

24 O wretched man that I am! who shall deliver me from the body of this death? 25 I thank God through Jesus Christ our Lord. So then with the mind I myself serve the law of God; but with the flesh the law of sin. (Rom 7:24-25)

We echo Paul as he cries out in wretched frustration at his inability to do the right thing. The more we want to do good, the more our flesh turns toward evil.

"O wretched man that I am!"

When we try to be right and pleasing to God by trying to obey the Commandments, we find only wretched misery and defeat.

"who shall deliver me from the body of this death?"

Because of sin dwelling in our flesh, we cannot please God by trying to keep God's Law. Saved or lost, the result is the same: wretched misery.

By Holy Spirit inspiration, Paul answers that wretched cry of who will deliver me from the body of this death.

Who?
Jesus!
That's who!

Our acceptance by God is no longer on the basis of how well we keep God's Law given through Moses. Instead, the truth is that we are accepted by Grace because of Jesus Christ!

17 For the law was given by Moses, but grace and truth came by Jesus Christ. (John 1:17)

We do not please God by obeying commandments, for if we try that approach, we are obligated to obey EVERY commandment, which is impossible for us.

10 For whosoever shall keep the whole law, and yet offend in one point, he is guilty of all. (James 2:10)

Instead of trying (unsuccessfully) to please God by keeping the Law, we in fact please Him by accepting and living our lives in the grace He has provided for us through faith in His Son, Jesus Christ!

Chapter 8

1 There is therefore now no condemnation to them which are in Christ Jesus, who walk not after the flesh, but after the Spirit. 2 For the law of the Spirit of life in Christ Jesus hath made me free from the law of sin and death. (Rom 8:1-2)

When you see a "therefore", it is referring back to what was just discussed. So, what was said that made Paul write "There is therefore now no condemnation to them which are in Christ Jesus"? The answer is that sin dwells in our bodies, our flesh, and that presence of evil drives us to commit sin, which brings condemnation because it breaks God's Law. But! A believer in Jesus is born-again, and has a new nature, a new one that does not sin.

The Apostle John wrote:
9 Whosoever is born of God doth not commit sin; for his seed remaineth in him: and he cannot sin, because he is born of God. (1 John 3:9)

Paul had previously written that the Spirit and the flesh are in combat with each other:

16 This I say then, Walk in the Spirit, and ye shall not fulfil the lust of the flesh. 17 For the flesh lusteth against the Spirit, and the Spirit against the flesh: and these are contrary the one to the other: so that ye cannot do the things that ye would. 18 But if ye be led of the Spirit, ye are not under the law. (Gal 5:16-18)

By the new nature, the born-again one we received from the Holy Spirit when we trusted in Jesus Christ, we are able to NOT sin.

3 For what the law could not do, in that it was weak through the flesh, God sending his own Son in the likeness of sinful flesh, and for sin, condemned sin in the flesh: 4 That the righteousness of the law might be fulfilled in us, who walk not after the flesh, but after the Spirit. (Rom 8:3-4)

The Law could not make us right with God because it depended on our actions done through our bodies which were tainted thoroughly with sin. Since we could not make ourselves right with God, God chose the only way that would make us right with Him – He sent Jesus! Jesus put on a body like ours, yet without the dreadful evil nature of sin that lives in us. He fulfilled the righteous requirements of the Law, something we could never do in ourselves, no matter how sincere or how hard we tried. When we trust in Jesus for our salvation, we are joined to Him; His righteousness in having obeyed the Law now gets credited to us so that we are counted as having that righteousness of the Law fulfilled in us too.

5 For they that are after the flesh do mind the things of the flesh; but they that are after the Spirit the things of the Spirit. 6 For to be carnally minded is death; but to be spiritually minded is life and peace. 7 Because the carnal mind is enmity against God: for it is not subject to the law of God, neither indeed can be. 8 So then they that are in the flesh cannot please God. 9 But ye are not in the flesh, but in the Spirit, if so be that the Spirit of God dwell in you. Now if any man have not the Spirit of Christ, he is none of his. 10 And if Christ be in you, the body is dead because of sin; but the Spirit is life because of righteousness. 11 But if the Spirit of him that raised up Jesus from the dead dwell in you, he that raised up Christ from the dead shall also quicken your mortal bodies by his Spirit that dwelleth in you. (Rom 8:5-11)

An important distinction is made in the verses above. We are told about "after the flesh" and "in the flesh", and also "after the Spirit" and "in the Spirit."

The word "after" is the Greek κατά kata which has many meanings, but the primary meaning here seems to be "according to". Here is that usage (from verse 5) from another translation:

5 For those who are according to the flesh set their minds on the things of the flesh, but those who are according to the Spirit, the things of the Spirit. (Rom 8:5 NASB)

The word "in" is the Greek word ἐν en which carries the idea of denoting a fixed position in place, time or state.

The unbeliever is "in" the flesh. That is his place or position, his HQ, if we could put it that way. His is a carnal mind, without faith in Jesus, and CANNOT please God.

6 But without faith it is impossible to please him [God] (Heb 11:6a)

The pattern of an unbeliever's life is that he acts "after" (or "according to") the impulse of the evil that is "in" his flesh.

But, a believer's mind is rooted in faith in Jesus, and that faith pleases God. Moreover, a believer is "in" the Spirit. When a person believes in Jesus, he is instantly born-again, and is washed and renewed by the indwelling presence of the Holy Spirit.

5 Not by works of righteousness which we have done, but according to his mercy he saved us, by the washing of regeneration, and renewing of the Holy Ghost; (Titus 3:5)

Those that are "in the flesh" cannot please God, but believers, being "in the Spirit", can -- and do -- please God. How do we know we who believe are "in the Spirit"? Simple. You are "in the Spirit" if you have the Holy Spirit.

13 In whom ye also trusted, after that ye heard the word of truth, the gospel of your salvation: in whom also after that ye believed, ye were sealed with that Holy Spirit of promise, 14 Which is the earnest of our inheritance until the redemption of the purchased possession, unto the praise of his glory. (Ephesians 1:13-13)

Every believer has the Holy Spirit. Every unbeliever does NOT have the Holy Spirit. That presence of the Holy Spirit is also proof, our "earnest", that one day, the believer will be resurrected and given a new glorified body like Christ's, and that evil nature in our flesh will be gone! When purchasing real estate, there is usually a down payment called "earnest money" that is given as a guarantee that the buyer will go through with the purchase of the property. By giving us the Holy Spirit as an "earnest", God is giving us His guarantee that He will go through with His purchase of us to bring us Home of Heaven.

12 Therefore, brethren, we are debtors, not to the flesh, to live after the flesh. 13 For if ye live after the flesh, ye shall die: but if ye through the Spirit do mortify the deeds of the body, ye shall live. 14 For as many as are led by the Spirit of God, they are the sons of God. 15 For ye have not received the spirit of bondage again to fear; but ye have received the Spirit of adoption, whereby we cry, Abba, Father. (Rom 8:12-15)

We are no longer obligated to follow the flesh, but we are instead led by the Spirit of God. We need to put to death the impulses which our sinful flesh drives us to do. We saw that in chapter 6 where Paul wrote, "Likewise reckon ye also yourselves to be dead indeed unto sin, but alive unto God through Jesus Christ our Lord." Jesus has purchased us with His blood.

In our flesh, we were slaves to sin. In the Spirit, we are free. It gets even better. We are not only God's "purchased possession" (Eph 1:14), but also His heirs, too. We're part of the family of God now. The intimacy of a relationship with God the Father is in contrast to the ownership of slavery. Believers are "adopted", which in Romans times meant you were as fully a part of the family as if you had been naturally born into it.

Our hearts cry out, "Abba!" I have heard that even today, little Hebrew children in Israel cry to their human father, "Abba! Abba!" How much more are we blessed to call God our Creator, Abba!

16 The Spirit itself beareth witness with our spirit, that we are the children of God: 17 And if children, then heirs; heirs of God, and joint-heirs with Christ; if so be that we suffer with him, that we may be also glorified together. 18 For I reckon that the sufferings of this present time are not worthy to be compared with the glory which shall be revealed in us. (Rom 8:16-18)

We cry out "Abba!" because the Holy Spirit is bearing witness in our hearts that our family relationship to God is real. Believers are truly God's children.

1 Behold, what manner of love the Father hath bestowed upon us, that we should be called the sons of God: therefore the world knoweth us not, because it knew him not. 2 Beloved, now are we the sons of God, and it doth not yet

appear what we shall be: but we know that, when he shall appear, we shall be like him; for we shall see him as he is. (1 John 3:1-2)

1 Be ye therefore followers of God, as dear children; 2 And walk in love, as Christ also hath loved us, and hath given himself for us an offering and a sacrifice to God for a sweetsmelling savour. (Ephesians 5:1-2)

As children of God, we have glory ahead of us we can scarce imagine now. However, the way to that glory has its pitfalls, for this present time has suffering for us. Ours is a fallen world that has troubles and death. There are sicknesses, calamities, and natural disasters. Earthquakes, hurricanes, tornadoes, floods, drought, plagues and more. There are man-made troubles caused by man's sinful nature. Persecution, crime, war, false imprisonment, torture and death happen to believers because of men who love their sin and hate God.

In the end, though, whatever suffering we may have here, whatever pierces our hearts and brings weeping to us now, all of that would be as nothing, unworthy to be compared to the glory God is bringing, a glory so great that the sufferings of this present time will fade like a nightmare when we first awaken from sleep.

19 For the earnest expectation of the creature waiteth for the manifestation of the sons of God. 20 For the creature was made subject to vanity, not willingly, but by reason of him who hath subjected the same in hope, 21 Because the creature itself also shall be delivered from the bondage of corruption into the glorious liberty of the children of God. 22 For we know that the whole creation groaneth and travaileth in pain together until now. 23 And not only they, but ourselves also, which have the

firstfruits of the Spirit, even we ourselves groan within ourselves, waiting for the adoption, to wit, the redemption of our body. 24 For we are saved by hope: but hope that is seen is not hope: for what a man seeth, why doth he yet hope for? 25 But if we hope for that we see not, then do we with patience wait for it. (Rom 8:19-25)

All creation is waiting with bated breath for the day that we, the children of God, will be revealed with Christ in our glorified resurrection bodies! When Adam sinned, God not only cursed the ground, but the ENTIRE UNIVERSE fell under that curse as well! That is why we have the humorous "Murphy's Law," which states, "If anything can go wrong, it will." That is the practical outworking of the curse: the entire Universe was cursed by God to work against Man. In the book of Revelation, when God makes a new heaven and a new earth, it is said that there will be no longer any curse (Rev 22:3).

But for now, the entire creation is awaiting our redemption, because when that day happens, it will signal that the creation itself will finally be redeemed as God makes a new heaven and a new earth.

Obviously, we are not there yet, so we have to wait with patient hope in our hearts, because that day IS coming! God has promised it, and God always keeps His promises!

26 Likewise the Spirit also helpeth our infirmities: for we know not what we should pray for as we ought: but the Spirit itself maketh intercession for us with groanings which cannot be uttered. 27 And he that searcheth the hearts knoweth what is the mind of the Spirit, because he maketh intercession for the saints according to the will of God. (Rom 8:26-27)

As we wait patiently for the hope of the day we will resurrected and finally be free of all the troubles of this present life, we get hard-pressed at time to even know how to pray. Our faith wavers at times, and we wonder why we are having all this trouble, and wish it would just go away. We are not left alone to face this life by ourselves. Verse 26 says, "Likewise the Spirit also helpeth our infirmities". When we face troubles, we at times do not even know how to pray about it. There are times we can only groan within ourselves, not having the words to express what is in our hearts and minds and emotions. It is then that the Holy Spirit steps in to help, for He understands the raw emotions we feel but do not know how to express, and so He prays, "with groanings which cannot be uttered." When the Spirit does that, Jesus Himself then intercedes for us before the Father's throne. In the midst of our infirmities, the entire Trinity cares and is involved!

28 And we know that all things work together for good to them that love God, to them who are the called according to his purpose. (Rom 8:28)

What a treasure of a verse! God causes everything to work together for good for us as believers. In this Church Age of Grace, we do not know just how good we have it. Nothing can touch our lives except that it has to filter through God the Father's hand first. Even when tragedies occur, God is at work to make them work together for our good.

29 For whom he did foreknow, he also did predestinate to be conformed to the image of his Son, that he might be the firstborn among many brethren. 30 Moreover whom he did predestinate, them he also called: and whom he called, them he also justified: and whom he justified, them he also glorified. (Rom 8:29-30)

We might ask, well, what is the good toward which God is working? In short, He is conforming us to the image of Christ. There is no greater good we can experience than to become more and more like Jesus. God has a destiny in mind for us, one He decided to make happen (a decision He made before He created the Universe) where we would be conformed to the image of Jesus so that we would be "many brothers and sisters" to Jesus, who would be the ultimate firstborn. As adopted children, believers have the same Father, and this means that when we as Christians call each other brother or sister, we really ARE brothers and sisters in God's personal family!

Having decided on our destiny from before the world began, God also called us to Himself through the preaching of the gospel of God's grace. When we responded by faith in Jesus, God the Father justified us. Remember, to justify mean to count someone as righteous, so when we trust in Jesus, the Father justified us, meaning He counted us as being as righteous as He Himself is. It doesn't get any better than that.

Lastly, Paul says that we who have been justified (and as believers we have), then it says God has glorified us. Wait a minute! Glorified? We still live in our flesh with its evil sin nature that drives us to commit sin. How can Paul say we have been glorified, meaning, it happened in the past tense.

The answer is that our salvation, and the day we will be resurrected into glorified bodies, is so sure in the mind of God, it is as certain as if it had already happened! We see again that same sureness and certainty in God's mind of our future, in Paul's letter to the Ephesians.

5 Even when we were dead in sins, hath quickened us together with Christ, (by grace ye are saved;) 6 And hath

raised us up together, and made us sit together in heavenly places in Christ Jesus: 7 That in the ages to come he might shew the exceeding riches of his grace in his kindness toward us through Christ Jesus. (Ephesians 2:5-7)

I think it safe to say that God's grace is vastly larger than our ability to comprehend it. We saw in Romans 5:20 where it says, "But where sin abounded, grace did much more abound." We also saw that the Greek for "much more abound" is ὑπερπερισσεύω hyperperisseuō, which means, "to abound beyond measure, abound exceedingly." God gives us SO much grace, it exceeds our ability to comprehend.

7 That in the ages to come he might shew the exceeding riches of his grace in his kindness toward us through Christ Jesus. (Eph 2:7)

We terribly underestimate God's grace so much. In the ages to come (and only God knows what THAT means!), He will use us, His children redeemed from the worse of sins, to show how awesomely full of grace He really is. We are His masterpiece of redemption. Is it any wonder that back in verse 18, it says, "For I reckon that the sufferings of this present time are not worthy to be compared with the glory which shall be revealed in us." It all comes back to His love for us, which we can't even fully understand:

19 May you experience the love of Christ, though it is too great to understand fully. Then you will be made complete with all the fullness of life and power that comes from God. (Eph 3:19 NLT).

31 What shall we then say to these things? If God be for us, who can be against us? (Romans 8:31)

What shall we say, indeed, to these things? I hope some of

this glory of God's redemptive grace touches your heart right now with awe and wonder! If God, the Supreme Being, the Creator, the all-powerful, all-knowing, all-wise King of kings and Lord of lords, the One who is Holy, Righteous, and who is Love, the true and living God, should be FOR us, who can possibly be against us? It is a rhetorical question: no one!

32 He that spared not his own Son, but delivered him up for us all, how shall he not with him also freely give us all things? 33 Who shall lay any thing to the charge of God's elect? It is God that justifieth. 34 Who is he that condemneth? It is Christ that died, yea rather, that is risen again, who is even at the right hand of God, who also maketh intercession for us. (Romans 8:32-34)

God loves us so much that He did not spare Jesus. Jesus is the greatest gift God could give us. His generosity is so great, that if He gave us His very best, then lesser things will be also freely available. Suppose a very rich man could easily give away a high-end and expensive sports car, would he balk in giving away a paper clip? If a man could do that, how much more so would God the Creator, who gave His Son who is infinitely more valuable than an expensive car, also freely give us lesser things? Such is the vastness of God's grace toward us who believe in Jesus.

35 Who shall separate us from the love of Christ? shall tribulation, or distress, or persecution, or famine, or nakedness, or peril, or sword? 36 As it is written, For thy sake we are killed all the day long; we are accounted as sheep for the slaughter. 37 Nay, in all these things we are more than conquerors through him that loved us. 38 For I am persuaded, that neither death, nor life, nor angels, nor principalities, nor powers, nor things present, nor things to come, 39 Nor height, nor depth, nor any other

creature, shall be able to separate us from the love of God, which is in Christ Jesus our Lord. (Rom 8:35-39)

Paul concludes this chapter with a broad statement of how secure a believer is in Jesus Christ. None of the troubles of life can separate us from God. Even though various trials can overtake us, including persecution and even death, we are more than conquerors. That expression means we win in the end.

However, that list of troubles is too short. Paul expands the possibilities of what may try to come between us and God in His love for us.

In the book, "Romans: The Gospel of God's Grace" by Alva McClain, the author explains what Paul is saying on this passage.

"He goes on to his final paean of praise! A Christian may take these words upon his lips without the least shadow of presumption. 'I am persuaded that nothing shall be able to separate me from the love of God!' Now he is going to search the universe for anything that could possibly separate us. He goes to the realm of death—he looks at it, he searches it. He says, 'There is nothing there that can separate us.' He then turns to the realm of life. He finds nothing there. He looks to the angelic or spiritual world. He finds nothing there among the good angels. He regards the other side—the principalities, representing Satan and all his hosts. There is nothing there!
"He then examines 'things present.' He then peers out into the future, 'things to come.' Who knows what those three words comprehend? Judgment—the ages of eternity! But he says, as he looks through the ages of eternity, 'There is nothing there!'
"But he does not stop. He scans the entire universe—the

heights and depths of the universe. He finds nothing there.
"One would have thought that Paul had covered everything but lest he may have missed something, he says, 'There is no creation that is able to separate us from the love of God.' Do you know what he means when he said that? He is considering the future, imagining the present creation passed away. He is anticipating that perhaps there will be infinite creations—on and on through the ages of eternity! He says, 'They all come up, as far as the prophetic eye can reach, and there is nothing in it all that can possibly separate us!'
"And he closes the passage as it began—'In Christ Jesus!'"

Chapter 9

1 I say the truth in Christ, I lie not, my conscience also bearing me witness in the Holy Ghost, 2 That I have great heaviness and continual sorrow in my heart. 3 For I could wish that myself were accursed from Christ for my brethren, my kinsmen according to the flesh: 4 Who are Israelites; to whom pertaineth the adoption, and the glory, and the covenants, and the giving of the law, and the service of God, and the promises; 5 Whose are the fathers, and of whom as concerning the flesh Christ came, who is over all, God blessed for ever. Amen. (Rom 9:1-5)

Having examined the overall need of mankind for the gospel, demonstrating that Jew and Gentile alike are guilty before God and therefore all people need the gospel, Paul takes time out to examine God's Chosen People, the children of Israel. Paul himself was a Jew, as was Peter. In the following passage, Paul recorded how he publicly rebuked Peter, speaking of their mutual Jewishness

14 But when I saw that they walked not uprightly according to the truth of the gospel, I said unto Peter before them all, If thou, being a Jew, livest after the manner of Gentiles, and not as do the Jews, why compellest thou the Gentiles to live as do the Jews? 15 We who are Jews by nature, and not sinners of the Gentiles, 16 Knowing that a man is not justified by the works of the law, but by the faith of Jesus Christ, even we have believed in Jesus Christ, that we might be justified by the faith of Christ, and not by the works of the law: for by the works of the law shall no flesh be justified. (Gal 2:14-16)

In another passage, Paul speaks of his Jewish ethnicity:

3 For we are the circumcision, which worship God in the spirit, and rejoice in Christ Jesus, and have no confidence in the flesh. 4 Though I might also have confidence in the flesh. If any other man thinketh that he hath whereof he might trust in the flesh, I more: 5 Circumcised the eighth day, of the stock of Israel, of the tribe of Benjamin, an Hebrew of the Hebrews; as touching the law, a Pharisee; 6 Concerning zeal, persecuting the church; touching the righteousness which is in the law, blameless. 7 But what things were gain to me, those I counted loss for Christ. (Phil 3:3-7)

Paul had such a heart burdened to share the gospel, and it grieved him that his fellow Israelites were missing out on the awesome salvation God had promised them! He wanted so intensely that they, too, along with the Gentiles, should come to faith in Jesus to be saved.

So, here in chapter 9, Paul gives voice to that burden, describing it as having 'great heaviness and continual sorrow in my heart." He so much wanted them to be saved! He even went so far as to say that, if it could save his fellow Jews, he would even have been willing to be "accursed" himself. In other words, he was willing to go to Hell if by doing so, his fellow Israelites could be saved! What love he had for them! He recounts the blessings and privileges they as a people had: "Who are Israelites; to whom pertaineth the adoption, and the glory, and the covenants, and the giving of the law, and the service of God, and the promises; Whose are the fathers, and of whom as concerning the flesh Christ came."

When on his missionary journeys and he came to a city, he would first seek out the local Jewish synagogue. As he wrote in Romans 1:16, the gospel was "to the Jew first, and also to the Greek." He was determined that the Jews would hear it first. It was only later that he finally gave up on his still-necked fellow Jews who blasphemed, and devoted himself to go to the Gentiles.

6 And when they opposed themselves, and blasphemed, he shook his raiment, and said unto them, Your blood be upon your own heads; I am clean; from henceforth I will go unto the Gentiles. (Acts 18:6)

The children of Israel had so much, but except for a believing remnant, they turned away from the promised Messiah when He came

6 Not as though the word of God hath taken none effect. For they are not all Israel, which are of Israel: 7 Neither, because they are the seed of Abraham, are they all children: but, In Isaac shall thy seed be called. 8 That is, They which are the children of the flesh, these are not the children of God: but the children of the promise are counted for the seed. 9 For this is the word of promise, At this time will I come, and Sara shall have a son.10 And not only this; but when Rebecca also had conceived by one, even by our father Isaac; 11 (For the children being not yet born, neither having done any good or evil, that the purpose of God according to election might stand, not of works, but of him that calleth;) 12 It was said unto her, The elder shall serve the younger. 13 As it

is written, Jacob have I loved, but Esau have I hated (Rom 9:6-13)

God (seen as "the angel of the Lord") made a promise to the patriarch Abraham after he obeyed God and was ready even to sacrifice his son:

15 And the angel of the LORD called unto Abraham out of heaven the second time, 16 And said, By myself have I sworn, saith the LORD, for because thou hast done this thing, and hast not withheld thy son, thine only son:17 That in blessing I will bless thee, and in multiplying I will multiply thy seed as the stars of the heaven, and as the sand which is upon the sea shore; and thy seed shall possess the gate of his enemies; 18 And in thy seed shall all the nations of the earth be blessed; because thou hast obeyed my voice. (Gen 18:15-18)

That promise continued on down through the family tree, from Abraham to Isaac, and from Isaac to Jacob. Jacob, grandson of Abraham, was renamed Israel after he had wrestled with God (Gen 32:28). The name "Israel" is a combination of the Hebrew words for "wrestle" and "God", sareta (you have wrestled) with God ('el).

Did God's promise fail for a blessing on Abraham through his "seed" (i.e. his children), what with the children of Israel rejecting Messiah? No, because not everyone born as a physical descendant would be part of that blessing. God has in mind also a spiritual "seed" in mind, as Paul wrote, "That is, They which are the children of the flesh, these are not the children of God: but the children of the promise are counted for the seed." God's promise of descendants would follow a lineage He chose, or "elected."

So, no, God's promise did NOT fail! Paul points out that God's promise would follow the lineage of the "seed" Abraham with which would be blessed, and that promised blessing was begun by going through Isaac. Abraham also had another son, Ishmael through the Egyptian woman, Hagar, but the promise of blessing did not go through him. When Isaac grew up, he in turn fathered two sons, Esau (the older) and Jacob. The blessing did not go through the eldest, Esau, but through the younger, Jacob.

Paul quoted from the Old Testament prophet Malachi when he wrote, "As it is written, Jacob have I loved, but Esau have I hated."

Let us see where Paul's reasoning goes with this.

14 What shall we say then? Is there unrighteousness with God? God forbid. 15 For he saith to Moses, I will have mercy on whom I will have mercy, and I will have compassion on whom I will have compassion. 16 So then it is not of him that willeth, nor of him that runneth, but of God that sheweth mercy. 17 For the scripture saith unto Pharaoh, Even for this same purpose have I raised thee up, that I might shew my power in thee, and that my name might be declared throughout all the earth. 18 Therefore hath he mercy on whom he will have mercy, and whom he will he hardeneth. (Romans 9:14-18)

Some people might say, that's not fair, implying God was wrong to pick those men (Isaac and Jacob) and not the others (Ismael and Esau). But, is it unfair, or wrong (i.e.

unrighteous)?

NO!

For one thing, it turns out neither Ishmael nor Esau, nor any of their descendants, were upright people. For instance, let's look at what Malachi wrote:

2 I have loved you, saith the LORD. Yet ye say, Wherein hast thou loved us? Was not Esau Jacob's brother? saith the LORD: yet I loved Jacob, 3 And I hated Esau, and laid his mountains and his heritage waste for the dragons of the wilderness. 4 Whereas Edom saith, We are impoverished, but we will return and build the desolate places; thus saith the LORD of hosts, They shall build, but I will throw down; and they shall call them, The border of wickedness, and, The people against whom the LORD hath indignation for ever. (Malachi 1:2-4)

The Edomites (i.e. descendants of Esau) were a wicked people. God did not exclude them for no good reason. While it is true that all men are sinners, Jacob came to trust in the Lord, and like Abraham his grandfather, his faith was reckoned for righteousness.

Now, that being said, we nonetheless have to realize that just because God does something for one person, does not mean He is obligated to do it for others. Paul again cited from the Old Testament when he quoted Scripture where Moses petitioned God to see God's glory:

18 And he said, I beseech thee, shew me thy glory. 19 And he said, I will make all my goodness pass before thee, and I

will proclaim the name of the LORD before thee; and will be gracious to whom I will be gracious, and will shew mercy on whom I will shew mercy. (Exodus 33:18-19)

For us today who are Christians, the practical application of this is that we may have a need, and when we see God provide wonderfully for someone else, it does not mean that He is obligated to do the same for us. For instance, we may have an illness, and someone else has that same illness, and if God miraculously heals them, it does not mean He is in any way obligated to do that same miracle for us.

In the same vein, whereas God may have mercy on one person's lack of faith, He may also choose to harden another in his unbelief. That was certainly true when He hardened Pharaoh's heart so that Pharaoh would not "let My people go."

As a side-note, Pharaoh hardened his own heart first several times, and then God hardened it for him.

Pharaoh hardening his own heart: Exodus 7:13; 8:15; 8:32; 9:34
God hardening Pharaoh's heart: Exodus 9:12; 10:27

God made sure Pharaoh reaped the consequences of his choices. It is like the old saying, "You made your bed, and now you will sleep in it."

For us today, there is still that principle operating, even as the Scripture says:

7 Be not deceived; God is not mocked: for whatsoever a

man soweth, that shall he also reap. (Gal 6:7)

So, in the final analysis, it is God's choice who to have mercy on, and who to harden. Yet, it is not inconsistent with His goodness. We saw how Esau was a faithless man lost in his wickedness. God chose wisely.

19 Thou wilt say then unto me, Why doth he yet find fault? For who hath resisted his will? 20 Nay but, O man, who art thou that repliest against God? Shall the thing formed say to him that formed it, Why hast thou made me thus? 21 Hath not the potter power over the clay, of the same lump to make one vessel unto honour, and another unto dishonour? 22 What if God, willing to shew his wrath, and to make his power known, endured with much longsuffering the vessels of wrath fitted to destruction: 23 And that he might make known the riches of his glory on the vessels of mercy, which he had afore prepared unto glory, 24 Even us, whom he hath called, not of the Jews only, but also of the Gentiles? 25 As he saith also in Osee, I will call them my people, which were not my people; and her beloved, which was not beloved. 26 And it shall come to pass, that in the place where it was said unto them, Ye are not my people; there shall they be called the children of the living God. (Romans 9:19-26)

Earlier in Romans, we saw various objections people could raise as to why they should not be judged. Now, here in Romans 9, there is a return to making objections, this time the objection being about God's reserving the right to choose whom He will, whether to have mercy upon whom He would have mercy, or to harden whom He will harden.

The objection is, "Thou wilt say then unto me, Why doth he yet find fault? For who hath resisted his will?" In other words, if God alone makes such choices, then how am I to blame if He chooses against me without any input from me? The answer to the question, as given by the Holy Spirit through Paul, is along the lines of, who do you think you are to question God like that? God is not simply higher than Man; He is INFINITELY higher than Man! He has thoughts and reasons way beyond our comprehension. He alone knows all the "ins and outs", the whole picture and all the details. We do not.

Paul turns to an object lesson all the people in his audience could understand. A potter would take a lump of clay, put it on a spinner, and slowly and gradually would shape and form some article for human use. He might make bowls for eating on, certainly an honorable use, or a chamber pot for human toilet needs, a dishonorable use (i.e. no one would want to eat off an article of pottery used as a toilet). The decision of what to make is solely the potter's choice, not the clay's.

God's choices are not random or chaotic. He has good reasons for the choices He makes. One choice God made was to delay pouring out His wrath on sinners. Why? Because He had in mind to mercifully bring about salvation for sinners, to reconcile sinful men to Himself through the Savior He was sending, Jesus the Christ/Messiah. If He had simply exercised His wrath, NONE of us would have been saved! God has the right to make the choices He makes, and our best response is to trust Him and that He wisely and graciously knows what He is doing.

God has called both Jew and Gentile to come to Jesus to be
saved by grace through faith. We need only look to the book
of Revelation to see that God's longsuffering (vs 22) will
come to an end, and He will finally bring about the wrath
He has delayed for so long.

Judgment delayed is not judgment denied.

Paul then refers to the book of Osee (Hosea) and shows
from it that God had in mind to not only saved the children
of Israel, but also the Gentiles.

**27 Esaias also crieth concerning Israel, Though the
number of the children of Israel be as the sand of the
sea, a remnant shall be saved: 28 For he will finish the
work, and cut it short in righteousness: because a short
work will the Lord make upon the earth. 29 And as
Esaias said before, Except the Lord of Sabaoth had left
us a seed, we had been as Sodoma, and been made like
unto Gomorrha. (Rom 9:27-29)**

In addressing this matter of God's choices, we find that
God's salvation came to both Jews and Gentiles, and yet
only a remnant of the people of Israel actually believed in
their Messiah Jesus. Isaiah prophesied that this would be the
case, that only a remnant of Israel would be saved. The rest
were placed under judgment for their rejection of Jesus with
a spiritual blindness (Rom 11:25).

**30 What shall we say then? That the Gentiles, which
followed not after righteousness, have attained to
righteousness, even the righteousness which is of faith.
31 But Israel, which followed after the law of**

righteousness, hath not attained to the law of righteousness. 32 Wherefore? Because they sought it not by faith, but as it were by the works of the law. For they stumbled at that stumblingstone; 33 As it is written, Behold, I lay in Sion a stumblingstone and rock of offence: and whosoever believeth on him shall not be ashamed. (Rom 9:30-33)

There is such a painful irony for Paul, a Jew, to write of his fellow Jews, that it would be primarily the Gentiles who would be saved, not his fellow Jews. The Gentiles responded to the gospel with faith, and received the imputed righteousness where God justifies the believer in Jesus. Most of the Jews did not respond by faith, but kept trying to be right with God by clinging to Moses and the Law, and so they failed to get God's righteousness. They would not accept Christ, but stumbled over Him.

A stumbling stone is an interesting thing. When we walk along a path, if we came to a boulder, we would not stumble (or trip) over it. It is too big and obvious. But, a small stone, one you would hardly notice, can catch your toes and make you stumble. The gospel of Jesus Christ is like that. It is so plain and simple, you would hardly think there is anything to it.

Some people say, "You mean, I can just believe in Jesus, and then go to heaven? That's it? That's all there is to it?"

You see? A stumbling stone. It is so simple and plain, people get indignant. When I shared the gospel with a woman at work, that quote I gave was pretty much her reaction. Then she said, "I can't believe that! I WON'T believe that!"

Her pride was offended. After all, she thought she was a pretty good person. She was confident that SHE would make it to Heaven, but no, those dirty sinners out there would not! Alas, if people take that reaction to their grave, there is no hope for them, only judgment and Hell. Yes, the simple message of the gospel is a stumbling stone.

On the gospel being a stumbling stone, there is also this verse:

11 And I, brethren, if I yet preach circumcision, why do I yet suffer persecution? then is the offence of the cross ceased. (Gal 5:11)

The Greek word for "offense" is σκάνδαλον skandalon, which means "any impediment placed in the way and causing one to stumble or fall, (a stumbling block, occasion of stumbling) i.e. a rock which is a cause of stumbling"

The Greek σκάνδαλον skandalon is the root word from which we get our English word "scandal." Yes, people are scandalized by the simplicity of the gospel! It offends their human pride.

Yet, if we do believe in Jesus, then we will not be ashamed when this life is over.

Chapter 10

1 Brethren, my heart's desire and prayer to God for Israel is, that they might be saved. 2 For I bear them record that they have a zeal of God, but not according to knowledge. 3 For they being ignorant of God's righteousness, and going about to establish their own righteousness, have not submitted themselves unto the righteousness of God. 4 For Christ is the end of the law for righteousness to every one that believeth. 5 For Moses describeth the righteousness which is of the law, That the man which doeth those things shall live by them. (Rom 10:1-5)

Bible teachers have described Romans chapters 9 through 11 this way:

Romans 9, Israel's past
Romans 10, Israel's present
Romans 11, Israel's future

We saw Israel's past in Romans 9. Now we turn our eyes in this chapter to see the present spiritual situation with God's ancient people, Israel.

Paul starts by describing his desire and prayer that his fellows among the children of Israel would be saved. We saw in chapter 2 how that the Jews, along with the Gentiles of the world, are guilty before God, which leads back to Romans 1:

16 For I am not ashamed of the gospel of Christ: for it is the power of God unto salvation to every one that believeth; to the Jew first, and also to the Greek. 17 For therein is the righteousness of God revealed from faith to faith: as it is written, The just shall live by faith. (Romans 1:16-17)

The Jews need to be saved because they are as guilty as everybody else, for they broke the commandments of God's Law, and were found guilty before God. Which commandment they broke is really irrelevant, as James wrote:

10 For whosoever shall keep the whole law, and yet offend in one point, he is guilty of all. (James 2:10)

Paul acknowledged his fellow Jews had zeal, but the tragedy is that their zeal was not based on the knowledge of the truth of the gospel. They kept on (and to this day, still do keep on) trying to be right with God – righteous – based on their human performance and obedience to the Law, never realizing that their best is not good enough, and never will be. They simply are ignorant of the righteousness of God that comes by grace through faith in the Messiah, Jesus of Nazareth. Being ignorant, they still keep trying to establish their own righteousness, a truly hopeless task, and do not submit to the righteousness that God offers to impute to them. Remember how we discussed the word impute, which is the Greek λογίζομαι logizomai, "to take an inventory"? God will impute His own righteousness to them, that is, count their "inventory" of righteousness as full, complete, and perfect if they will but trust in Jesus Christ.

Paul then sums things up by writing, "For Christ is the end of the law for righteousness to every one that believeth." Once a person trusts in Jesus Christ, there is no more trying to be "good enough" by obedience to the Commandments of the Law (Not just the Ten Commandments, but all 613 of them, the entire Law). Christ Himself is the end of following the Law to be right with God. When you have Christ, you don't need any more efforts to be right with God, because in Christ you ARE right with God!

6 But the righteousness which is of faith speaketh on this wise, Say not in thine heart, Who shall ascend into heaven? (that is, to bring Christ down from above:) 7 Or, Who shall descend into the deep? (that is, to bring up Christ again from the dead.) 8 But what saith it? The word is nigh thee, even in thy mouth, and in thy heart: that is, the word of faith, which we preach; 9 That if thou shalt confess with thy mouth the Lord Jesus, and shalt believe in thine heart that God hath raised him from the dead, thou shalt be saved. 10 For with the heart man believeth unto righteousness; and with the mouth confession is made unto salvation. 11 For the scripture saith, Whosoever believeth on him shall not be ashamed. (Romans 10:6-11)

Paul then says that we do not have to ascend to two extremes, the heights of heaven nor plumb the depths of the grave, to find and obtain the righteousness that comes by faith. Unlike the Law with its requirements on strict behavior with people striving with their best behavior to be right with God, we don't have to make all that effort at all. That righteousness we need is within reach, right at our fingertips. It is the word of faith, as Paul told the Philippian jailer, "Believe on the Lord Jesus Christ and you will be saved" (Acts 16:31)
Paul defined the gospel for us in another place:

3 For I delivered unto you first of all that which I also received, how that Christ died for our sins according to the scriptures; 4 And that he was buried, and that he rose again the third day according to the scriptures: (1 Cor 15:3-4)

When we believe the gospel, we are told here in Romans told, "That if thou shalt confess with thy mouth the Lord Jesus, and shalt believe in thine heart that God hath raised him from the dead, thou shalt be saved." Believing in Jesus includes the realization that He was not only a man. When we "confess ... the Lord Jesus", we are confessing that He is the Son of God.

The Apostle John wrote, "Who is he that overcometh the world, but he that believeth that Jesus is the Son of God?" (1 John 5:5)

Yes, the resurrection is SO important, that it is an essential part of believing the gospel so that we can be saved. At this point in Romans, Paul emphasizes the resurrection as part of believing to be saved, "shalt believe in thine heart that God hath raised him from the dead." No faith in the resurrection, no salvation. But! When we do believe in Jesus, the Son of God who died for our sins and rose again the third day, then when it comes to our entrance to Heaven, we will not be ashamed.

12 For there is no difference between the Jew and the Greek: for the same Lord over all is rich unto all that call upon him. 13 For whosoever shall call upon the name of the Lord shall be saved. 14 How then shall they call on him in whom they have not believed? and how shall they believe in him of whom they have not heard? and how shall they hear without a preacher? 15 And how shall they preach, except they be sent? as it is written, How beautiful are the feet of them that preach the gospel of peace, and bring glad tidings of good things! (Rom 10:12-15)

Anyone who believes in Jesus, whether Jew or Gentile, will be saved. God makes no difference between them. All racial, societal and class distinctions are removed in Christ.

28 There is neither Jew nor Greek, there is neither bond nor free, there is neither male nor female: for ye are all one in

Christ Jesus. (Gal 3:28)
11 Where there is neither Greek nor Jew, circumcision nor uncircumcision, Barbarian, Scythian, bond nor free: but Christ is all, and in all. (Col 3:11)
13 But now in Christ Jesus ye who sometimes were far off are made nigh by the blood of Christ. 14 For he is our peace, who hath made both one, and hath broken down the middle wall of partition between us; (Eph 2:13-14)

Anyone at all who calls upon the name of Jesus for salvation will be saved. So, if everyone who calls upon Jesus will be saved, it then becomes important to make sure that the gospel goes out so that people can hear about Jesus. Spreading the gospel is close to God's heart for all men to be saved, and Paul quote from the Old Testament about it, "How beautiful are the feet of them that preach the gospel of peace, and bring glad tidings of good things."

The gospel really is Good News!

16 But they have not all obeyed the gospel. For Esaias saith, Lord, who hath believed our report? 17 So then faith cometh by hearing, and hearing by the word of God. 18 But I say, Have they not heard? Yes verily, their sound went into all the earth, and their words unto the ends of the world. 19 But I say, Did not Israel know? First Moses saith, I will provoke you to jealousy by them that are no people, and by a foolish nation I will anger you. 20 But Esaias is very bold, and saith, I was found of them that sought me not; I was made manifest unto them that asked not after me. 21 But to Israel he saith, All day long I have stretched forth my hands unto a disobedient and gainsaying people. (Rom 10:16-21)

However much the gospel does go out, though, the sad truth is that not everyone who hears it is going to believe it. Isaiah

lamented, "Lord, who hath believed our report?"
When Paul wrote that faith comes by hearing God's Word
and that Word has to be accompanied by faith. Israel heard,
but they did not believe it. God chose to use the Gentiles
who did believe to make jealous Israel which did not believe.
The jealousy would be in the Jews seeing Gentiles, whom
they despises, demonstrating spiritual gifts from THEIR
God!

It did little good. The Jews as a nation rejected Jesus, but the
Gentiles received Him. You can feel God's displeasure when
He had Isaiah write, "All day long I have stretched forth my
hands unto a disobedient and gainsaying people."

The Jews back then, and to this very day, are rebellious and
stiff-necked, and while a remnant of individual Jews
thankfully have responded to the gospel, they as a people do
not believe in Jesus!

Chapter 11

1 I say then, Hath God cast away his people? God forbid. For I also am an Israelite, of the seed of Abraham, of the tribe of Benjamin. 2 God hath not cast away his people which he foreknew. Wot ye not what the scripture saith of Elias? how he maketh intercession to God against Israel, saying, 3 Lord, they have killed thy prophets, and digged down thine altars; and I am left alone, and they seek my life. 4 But what saith the answer of God unto him? I have reserved to myself seven thousand men, who have not bowed the knee to the image of Baal. 5 Even so then at this present time also there is a remnant according to the election of grace. 6 And if by grace, then is it no more of works: otherwise grace is no more grace. But if it be of works, then is it no more grace: otherwise work is no more work. (Rom 11:1-6)

Looking back at chapters 9 and 10, we see how Israel did not believe it when Messiah came as promised. God has, through the prophet Daniel, even told them the very exact day that Messiah would appear! In the startling Prophecy of the Seventy Weeks in Daniel chapter 9, the destiny of the children of Israel was given.

24 Seventy weeks are determined upon thy people and upon thy holy city, to finish the transgression, and to make an end of sins, and to make reconciliation for iniquity, and to bring in everlasting righteousness, and to seal up the vision and prophecy, and to anoint the most Holy. 25 Know therefore and understand, that from the going forth of the commandment to restore and to build Jerusalem unto the Messiah the Prince shall be seven weeks, and threescore and two weeks: the street shall be built again, and the wall, even in troublous times. (Dan 9:24-25)

These "weeks" are weeks of years, meaning, one of these prophetic weeks equals seven years, where each year = 360 days. The starting point for the countdown would be "from the going forth of the commandment to restore and to build Jerusalem." At the time this prophecy was given, Daniel and Israel were in captivity in Babylon, and Jerusalem was destroyed. Some have believed that starting point happened with Ezra, but he was given a mandate to rebuild the temple (Ezra 1:1-3), not the city. It was rather Nehemiah who has later given the mandate "to restore and to build Jerusalem." It happened in Nehemiah 2:1-8 in 445 BC.

The prophecy states that from the starting point "unto the Messiah the Prince shall be seven weeks, and threescore and two weeks". This timeframe is a total of 69 "weeks", or 483 years. Scholars pinpointed the starting date through the calendar of the reign of Artaxerxes, and also the time on the Hebrew calendar.

What all of this means is that, from that starting point in time for when King Artaxerxes gave Nehemiah the mandate to rebuild Jerusalem, the exact time Messiah would show up came to what we call Palm Sunday when Jesus entered Jerusalem on the back of a donkey and the people praised Him crying out, "Hosanna!".

The people of Israel, had they consulted their own prophecies, could have – and should have – known that Jesus was their Messiah.

With all their inexcusable rejection, the question the Apostle Paul raises is whether God is done and over with all His people Israel? Surely, they would have all deserved it. But, no, God has NOT discarded them! Paul wrote, "God hath not cast away his people which he foreknew" and points out that he himself was a one of the believers in Jesus, "For I also am an Israelite, of the seed of Abraham, of the tribe of Benjamin."

While God did pass judgment on Israel for their unbelief, yet He reserved even to this day a remnant that would believe. Paul teaches us that the decision to have a believing remnant is God's choice, a decision made by grace and not according to the works of His people Israel. Grace and works are incompatible and mutually exclusive. We cannot mix them. The moment we add works, it is no longer grace.

7 What then? Israel hath not obtained that which he seeketh for; but the election hath obtained it, and the rest were blinded. 8 (According as it is written, God hath given them the spirit of slumber, eyes that they should not see, and ears that they should not hear;) unto this day. 9 And David saith, Let their table be made a snare, and a trap, and a stumbling block, and a recompence unto them: 10 Let their eyes be darkened, that they may not see, and bow down their back alway. 11 I say then, Have they stumbled that they should fall? God forbid: but rather through their fall salvation is come unto the Gentiles, for to provoke them to jealousy. 12 Now if the fall of them be the riches of the world, and the diminishing of them the riches of the Gentiles; how much more their fulness? 13 For I speak to you Gentiles, inasmuch as I am the apostle of the Gentiles, I magnify mine office: 14 If by any means I may provoke to emulation them which are my flesh, and might save some of them. 15 For if the casting away of them be the reconciling of the world, what shall the receiving of them be, but life from the dead? (Rom 11:7-15)

Paul makes the troublesome observation that Israel ended up not obtaining the promised Messiah, but only the ones God chose obtained Jesus, and God blinded the rest with a spiritual blindness. King David wrote in the Psalms of that judgment upon them, saying what happened to them from God was "recompense." The Greek word for "recompense" is ἀνταπόδομα antapodoma, which means "the thing paid back." God was paying them back for their evil unbelief. Here is another Scripture written to the Hebrew people where God will recompense:

30 For we know him that hath said, Vengeance belongeth unto me, I will recompense, saith the Lord. And again, The Lord shall judge his people. 31 It is a fearful thing to fall into the hands of the living God. (Hebrews 10:30-31)

The children of Israel stumbled and fell. However, God had a plan from eternity past that when Israel fell, salvation would come to the Gentiles. Why? Because He wanted to make Israel jealous over how the much-despised Gentiles had obtained the Messiah that the Jews had been promised but did not obtain because of their own stubborn stiff necks. Paul then brings up an interesting contrast. If the riches of salvation came to the Gentiles of the world through Israel's fall, how much more will there be a rich blessing when Israel finally returns to the Lord?

Paul wanted so much for his fellow Israelites to come to saving faith in Jesus. He wrote, "If by any means I may provoke to emulation them which are my flesh, and might save some of them." If he couldn't win all of them to Christ, he hoped fervently that he could reach at least some of them.

16 For if the firstfruit be holy, the lump is also holy: and if the root be holy, so are the branches. 17 And if some of the branches be broken off, and thou, being a wild olive tree, wert graffed in among them, and with them partakest of the root and fatness of the olive tree; 18

Boast not against the branches. But if thou boast, thou bearest not the root, but the root thee. 19 Thou wilt say then, The branches were broken off, that I might be graffed in. 20 Well; because of unbelief they were broken off, and thou standest by faith. Be not highminded, but fear: 21 For if God spared not the natural branches, take heed lest he also spare not thee. 22 Behold therefore the goodness and severity of God: on them which fell, severity; but toward thee, goodness, if thou continue in his goodness: otherwise thou also shalt be cut off. 23 And they also, if they abide not still in unbelief, shall be graffed in: for God is able to graff them in again. 24 For if thou wert cut out of the olive tree which is wild by nature, and wert graffed contrary to nature into a good olive tree: how much more shall these, which be the natural branches, be graffed into their own olive tree? (Rom 11:16-24)

Paul then turns to nature for object lessons to illustrate what happened spiritually with Israel and the Gentiles. First he speaks of "firstfruits" and a "lump". This has to do with the firstfruits of the grain which was offered to God. In this context, the lump is speaking of the first portion of the dough, from which sacred loaves were to be prepared for temple service. So, there is a foundation, so to speak, of a batch of bread dough (i.e. the lump) from which the first portion of it (i.e. the firstfruits) were prepared. Paul is saying if the first part of what came out of the main batch is holy, then it follows that the lump from which it came is also holy.

Then Paul turns to using olive trees as a spiritual object lesson. Certainly the Romans knew all about olive trees, as they were very common throughout the Mediterranean region including Italy. Paul uses two kinds of olive trees in his illustration: a cultivated olive tree, and one that grew wild. God cultivated His people Israel, helping them along the way, wanting to use them as His witnesses of who He is and what He could do, and how people could find forgiveness of sins. But when Israel rejected that course of responsibility, God set them aside for a season, it being illustrated by the breaking off some of the branches (representing Israel) from the cultivated olive tree. Then, illustrating how God brought salvation to the Gentiles, branches from the wild olive tree (representing the Gentiles) were grafted into the cultivated tree (from which sprang Israel.) Therefore, the Church Age believing Gentiles, along with the remnant of believing Jews, are reaping the benefit of the promises originally given to Israel.

However, Paul warns that the Gentile believer should not be "highminded", saying, "For if God spared not the natural branches, take heed lest he also spare not thee." This is not a warning that someone who is a Gentile believer can lose their salvation. Rather, it is saying that the Gentiles do not have a locked-in position in God's promises originally given to Israel. Just as God broke off some of the Jewish branches, He can in His purposes also re-graft them back into the cultivated tree.

25 For I would not, brethren, that ye should be ignorant of this mystery, lest ye should be wise in your own conceits; that blindness in part is happened to Israel, until the fulness of the Gentiles be come in. 26 And so all Israel shall be saved: as it is written, There shall come out of Sion the Deliverer, and shall turn away ungodliness from Jacob: 27 For this is my covenant unto them, when I shall take away their sins. 28 As concerning the gospel, they are enemies for your sakes: but as touching the election, they are beloved for the fathers' sakes. 29 For the gifts and calling of God are without repentance. (Rom 11:25-29)

Paul started this chapter saying that God had not cast away His people Israel. Yes, He placed a spiritual blindness on them as judgment, but that blindness is not forever. God's purposes included saving Gentiles, too. The phrase "the fulness of the Gentiles" occurs in vs 25. Apparently, God has in His purposes set a certain number of Gentiles to be saved in this Church Age. When that number is reached, the Church shall be withdrawn from this world in the prophesied Rapture of the Church, ending the Church Age. When that happens, the judgment of blindness of the hearts and minds of the children of Israel will be removed. Suddenly, they will understand who Jesus truly is, their promised Messiah, and they will finally believe in Him as vs 26 says, "And so all Israel shall be saved". Jesus the Deliverer will come out of Zion to fulfill the promise of God to them to take away their sins.

Currently, the people of Israel are enemies of the cross of Jesus, spiritually blinded to Him. Yet, God has chosen them, and hence their name "the Chosen People." When the Rapture happens, they once again become God's Chosen people, and even though they currently reject Jesus, God remembers His promises, and will fulfill them. Why? Because "the gifts and calling of God are without repentance". God called them, and gave them gifts. The things God gave the children of Israel, such as the land of Israel, are theirs forever, for they are "without repentance", meaning without a change of mind, i.e. irrevocable. When God makes a promise, He keeps that promise.

30 For as ye in times past have not believed God, yet have now obtained mercy through their unbelief: 31 Even so have these also now not believed, that through your mercy they also may obtain mercy. 32 For God hath concluded them all in unbelief, that he might have mercy upon all. (Rom 11:30-32)

The Romans "in times past" had not believed in the true God, but had borrowed all the ancient Greek gods and renamed them for Roman purposes. Zeus became Jupiter, Aphrodite became Venus. Heracles became Hercules, and so on. Yet, whether Greek or Roman, it was all idolatry. God had mercy upon the Gentile Romans (and us today who are not of Jewish descent). The mercy that God has shown the Gentile world will one day, after the time "the fulness of the Gentiles" comes in, be turned around and shown to Israel. Hence, vs 26 saying "And so all Israel shall be saved". Yes, with the spiritual blindness removed, God in His mercy will bring salvation to all Israel and the Gentiles so that all, being guilty of sin, can all receive forgiveness for sin.

33 O the depth of the riches both of the wisdom and knowledge of God! how unsearchable are his judgments, and his ways past finding out! 34 For who hath known the mind of the Lord? or who hath been his counseller? 35 Or who hath first given to him, and it shall be recompensed unto him again? 36 For of him, and through him, and to him, are all things: to whom be glory for ever. Amen. (Rom 11:33-36)

Paul ends this look into Israel with a doxology praising God's wisdom, that His ways are far deeper than we could ever dream. No one has ever given God advice because He truly knows everything. In the end, everything will one day abound to the glory of God!

Chapter 12

1 I beseech you therefore, brethren, by the mercies of God, that ye present your bodies a living sacrifice, holy, acceptable unto God, which is your reasonable service. 2 And be not conformed to this world: but be ye transformed by the renewing of your mind, that ye may prove what is that good, and acceptable, and perfect, will of God. (Rom 12:1-2)

The Old Testament had sacrifices where an animal was killed to make temporary atonement for a person's sins.

1 For the law having a shadow of good things to come, and not the very image of the things, can never with those sacrifices which they offered year by year continually make the comers thereunto perfect. 2 For then would they not have ceased to be offered? because that the worshippers once purged should have had no more conscience of sins. 3 But in those sacrifices there is a remembrance again made of sins every year. 4 For it is not possible that the blood of bulls and of goats should take away sins. (Heb 10:1-4)

The animal sacrifices only temporarily covered sins. It would be like sweeping a dirty floor, and sweeping all the gathered dirt into a pile in the middle of the floor. Then, take a rug and throw it over the pile of dirt. The rug does not take away the dirt, but only covers it up.

But when Christ came, the sins were no longer merely covered up with sacrifices of bulls and goats like in the Law of Moses, It was only when Christ came that those temporary sacrifices were put away because Christ was the Lamb of God that takes away the sins of the world. In our illustration, it would be like taking the rug off the pile of swept-up dirt, and then using a vacuum cleaner and mop and bucket, and actually removing the dirt altogether. The floor would not merely "look" clean (i.e. with a rug covering the dirt), but would actually BE clean!

In light of what Christ has done for us in His permanent sacrifice to take away our sins, what should our response be in our day-to-day life? Paul answers that by saying "that ye present your bodies a living sacrifice, holy, acceptable unto God, which is your reasonable service." How do we do this? In part, we need to remember what Scripture says about us, that we are to no longer use our bodies for sinful purposes.

15 Know ye not that your bodies are the members of Christ? shall I then take the members of Christ, and make them the members of an harlot? God forbid. 16 What? know ye not that he which is joined to an harlot is one body? for two, saith he, shall be one flesh. 17 But he that is joined unto the Lord is one spirit. 18 Flee fornication. Every sin that a man doeth is without the body; but he that committeth fornication sinneth against his own body. 19 What? know ye not that your body is the temple of the Holy Ghost which is in you, which ye have of God, and ye are not your own? 20 For ye are bought with a price: therefore glorify God in your body, and in your spirit, which are God's. (1 Cor 6:15-20)

Now, that portion describes the use of our bodies. While that passage describes the wrongful use of our bodies for sexual immorality, it also applies to any other wrongful use of the body, such as alcohol or drug abuse.

After writing of how to serve God with our bodies, Paul then speaks to how to serve God with our minds.

In his letter to the Philippians, Paul wrote:

6 Be careful for nothing; but in everything by prayer and

supplication with thanksgiving let your requests be made known unto God. 7 And the peace of God, which passeth all understanding, shall keep your hearts and minds through Christ Jesus. 8 Finally, brethren, whatsoever things are true, whatsoever things are honest, whatsoever things are just, whatsoever things are pure, whatsoever things are lovely, whatsoever things are of good report; if there be any virtue, and if there be any praise, think on these things. 9 Those things, which ye have both learned, and received, and heard, and seen in me, do: and the God of peace shall be with you. (Phil 4:6-9)

Now, in this Romans 12 passage, we find an interesting contrast for our minds between passive and active thinking. He writes, "And be not conformed to this world: but be ye transformed by the renewing of your mind." The word "conformed" is passive. It is the idea of a lump of clay being squeezed into whatever shape the potter desires. In contrast, the word "transformed" is active. It is the potter acting to make the clay into whatever shape he desires.

As an illustration, consider you and I are in a rowboat in a river with a current. We desire to go upstream, for we know we really need to go that way, but we make no effort to do so. As a result, we allow the stream to carry us downstream to where we do not want to go.

That is the passive word "conformed", which is us making no effort to use the oars to propel ourselves against the current. In this illustration, the downstream current is the desires of the world, the flesh and the devil, to carry us away from God our Savior.

In contrast is the word "transformed", where we resist the current of the world, the flesh and the devil. We put our oars in the water of the river, and row upstream to where we need to go to walk with God our Savior.

Now, this is not about our salvation, that we should make effort or else we are not saved. No, no, a thousand times, No! This is about our walk with the Lord in our lifetime, and how to please Him with our lives so that what we are doing is holy and acceptable to Him. It is like what Paul wrote to the Ephesians:

1 Be ye therefore followers of God, as dear children; 2 And walk in love, as Christ also hath loved us, and hath given himself for us an offering and a sacrifice to God for a sweetsmelling savour. 3 But fornication, and all uncleanness, or covetousness, let it not be once named among you, as becometh saints; 4 Neither filthiness, nor foolish talking, nor jesting, which are not convenient: but rather giving of thanks. (Eph 5:1-4)

Now, how exactly, are we to be "transformed"? It is all well and good to illustrate with putting oars in the water, but what does this look like in practical terms? Paul answers it this way: "the renewing of your mind." The Greek word for "renewing' is ἀνακαίνωσις anakainōsis. It means, a renewal, renovation, complete change for the better.

The best way to have a "complete change for the better" is to go to God's Word.

17 Sanctify them through thy truth: thy word is truth. (John 17:17)

11 Thy word have I hid in mine heart, that I might not sin against thee. (Ps 119:11)

105 Thy word is a lamp unto my feet, and a light unto my path. (Ps 119:105)

15 Study to shew thyself approved unto God, a workman that needeth not to be ashamed, rightly dividing the word of truth. (2 Tim 2:15)

3 For I say, through the grace given unto me, to every man that is among you, not to think of himself more highly than he ought to think; but to think soberly, according as God hath dealt to every man the measure of faith. 4 For as we have many members in one body, and all members have not the same office: 5 So we, being many, are one body in Christ, and every one members one of another. (Rom 12:3-5)

Living as people who have been saved by the unmerited, undeserved grace of God, we have no grounds for boasting.

8 For by grace are ye saved through faith; and that not of yourselves: it is the gift of God: 9 Not of works, lest any man should boast. (Eph 2:8-9)

So, when evaluating ourselves, let us not get "uppity airs" about who we are. God may choose to use us in a great way, but let it not become a season of pride. Rather, we need to keep a humble spirit about it. One such way God may choose to use us is by the exercise of the spiritual gift He gives every believer upon being saved and born-again by the Holy Spirit. A spiritual gift is a supernatural "talent" (different from a natural talent) given by the Holy Spirit as He deems best and wisest for each believer to have. The purpose for these spiritual gifts is expressed by Paul in his letter to the Ephesians, "For the perfecting of the saints, for the work of the ministry, for the edifying of the body of Christ" (Eph 4:11)

We who believe are members of the body of Christ, and just

as in a human body, not every part has the same function, so we each individually contribute to the body as a whole.

6 Having then gifts differing according to the grace that is given to us, whether prophecy, let us prophesy according to the proportion of faith; 7 Or ministry, let us wait on our ministering: or he that teacheth, on teaching; 8 Or he that exhorteth, on exhortation: he that giveth, let him do it with simplicity; he that ruleth, with diligence; he that sheweth mercy, with cheerfulness. (Rom 12:6-8)

Here in Romans, Paul describes some of the spiritual gifts. Whatever gift we as individuals as members of the body of Christ have, they are a gift of grace from God. We don't deserve them, and so our attitude should be humble as we use them.

First mentioned is the gift of prophesying. It is important to note here the roles of a prophet and a priest.

A prophet took the things of God and gave them to the people.
A priest took the things of the people, and gave them to God.

It has been said that a prophet did two things: foretelling, and forthtelling.

Forthtelling was a function of exhorting the people to turn from their sins back to God.

Foretelling was the role of a prophet to tell of things to come in the future. At the time Paul wrote the letter to the Romans, the book of Revelation, which shows the future, had not yet been written. Paul himself wrote many passages in his letters where he did exactly that, namely, write prophecies about the future. We see this in his describing the future in Philippians chapter 2, and his two letters to the Thessalonians, and in his letters to his young protégé, Timothy.

However, with the completion of the writing of the book of Revelation, there are no more prophets today and there is no more foretelling the future, because everything God wanted us to know about the future is already revealed to us in His written Word, the Scriptures of the Bible.

The second gift described in this chapter is ministry. It is a gift of serving, of being a helper where help is needed. People with this gift feel a joy in being helpful, and it is not at all one of drudgery.

Then Paul describes the gift of teaching. This gift enables a believer to open the Word of God to people, and make it simple and understandable to others, and shows how it is applicable to situations.

Next is exhortation. It was said that forthtelling, that is, exhortation, was one of the roles of a prophet. While there are no more prophets, exhortation lives on in people with this gift. An exhorter calls people to turn from their sins and live righteously in their walk with the Lord Jesus. How we need the exhorters God has gifted!

Then there is the gift of giving. This is a gift of grace whereby someone hears of a need, and gives materially and generously to meet that need. Often God will materially bless someone with that gift so that they will have the resources to give away to meet needs.

Next Paul describes the gift of ruling. This is the gift of the overseer, a person with leadership in the church that helps lead the people, a deacon or an elder.

17 Let the elders that rule well be counted worthy of double honour, especially they who labour in the word and doctrine. (1 Tim 4:17)

Last, Paul describes the gift of mercy showing. This is the gift that enables someone to be gentle with those who are hurting and have an understanding heart to minister to them. A woman I knew from church years ago had this gift. She was part of a team that met with people after the church service when coffee and snacks were served, and would hand out brochures for the church that told what the church's ministries were, etc. A man who knew her told me once that she handled the "EGRs." I was puzzled. "EGRs"? He smiled and explained, "Extra Grace Required." From his point of view, there were people who were such, shall we say, difficult people that others might turn away from them, but she handled them with gentle love and grace. The mercy-shower is often the person to whom people who are hurting will turn, someone who give them a listening ear for their burdens. Such is the grace of Jesus.

9 Let love be without dissimulation. Abhor that which is evil; cleave to that which is good. 10 Be kindly affectioned one to another with brotherly love; in honour preferring one another; (Rom 12:9-10)

Paul begins a series of short but concise admonitions on how to live as Christians.

Dissimulation is an interesting word. It means hypocrisy. If we are to love (Greek ἀγάπη agape) one another as Christ loved us, let that love be sincere, not faked or hypocritical.

We need to hate evil, but cling to good. This is particularly applicable to our entertainment where we have a choice to make. For example, do we watch movies that are, well, evil?

Kindly affectioned (Greek φιλόστοργος philostorgos) means the love between parents and their children; as applied to Christians, we are to exercise brotherly love (the Greek φιλαδελφία Philadelphia), which in the NT means the love which Christians cherish for each other as brethren. Because each Christian has been adopted by God the Father as one of His legal children, we who believe in Jesus share the same Father, which makes us really siblings in God's family. Is it any wonder that Christians call one another "brother", or "sister"?

Paul next says, "in honour preferring one another." This is a picture of valuing other believers greatly, such that we to go before them to show the way. Imagine a great mansion of a noble with many servants, and a guest of great importance, perhaps a prince or princess arrives. The servant leads the way to the mansion's lord, showing the arrived guest how honored they all are by the guest's presence. Paul wants us as believers to honor one another that way. In a way, the idea of a guest entering our home being a prince or princess is not at all far-fetched. Because every believer is adopted legally into the family of God as His children, well, that means each believer is a child of God, and that in turn means each believer really IS a prince or princess of highest royal standing, the child of the King of kings!

11 Not slothful in business; fervent in spirit; serving the Lord; (Rom 12:11)

In our business dealings, perhaps as an employee for a company, let's give our employer honest work for our pay, not sloth (i.e. laziness). Why? Because God wants us to be fervent, full of excitement, because we are really serving God when we work for someone.

5 Servants, be obedient to them that are your masters according to the flesh, with fear and trembling, in singleness of your heart, as unto Christ; 6 Not with eyeservice, as menpleasers; but as the servants of Christ, doing the will of God from the heart; 7 With good will doing service, as to the Lord, and not to men: (Eph 6:5-7)

In that ancient city of Rome, where one out of every three inhabitants were slaves, this was particularly important. "Eyeservice" means, working only when the boss is looking.

12 Rejoicing in hope; patient in tribulation; continuing instant in prayer; 13 Distributing to the necessity of saints; given to hospitality. (Rom 12:12-13)

For the Christian, this life is not everything. We have the unshakable hope of resurrection wherein we will one day be clothed by God in perfect immortal bodies. Knowing this, we then can patiently face troubles as they come. We are to be ready always to pray, whatever life brings our way.

If a brother or sister in Christ has need, we need to help them in their need, food, clothing, whatever.

15 If a brother or sister be naked, and destitute of daily food, 16 And one of you say unto them, Depart in peace, be ye warmed and filled; notwithstanding ye give them not those things which are needful to the body; what doth it profit? (James 2:15-17)

16 Hereby perceive we the love of God, because he laid down his life for us: and we ought to lay down our lives for the brethren. 17 But whoso hath this world's good, and seeth his brother have need, and shutteth up his bowels of compassion from him, how dwelleth the love of God in him? 18 My little children, let us not love in word, neither in

tongue; but in deed and in truth. (1 John 3:16-18)

If someone comes to our house, we should in love show them hospitality, freely giving because God has freely given to us.

2 Be not forgetful to entertain strangers: for thereby some have entertained angels unawares. (Hebrews 13:2)

Yet, if someone comes to our home bringing an antichrist message, we are NOT to show hospitality to them:

10 If there come any unto you, and bring not this doctrine, receive him not into your house, neither bid him God speed: 11 For he that biddeth him God speed is partaker of his evil deeds. (2 John 10-11)

14 Bless them which persecute you: bless, and curse not. 15 Rejoice with them that do rejoice, and weep with them that weep. 16 Be of the same mind one toward another. Mind not high things, but condescend to men of low estate. Be not wise in your own conceits. (Rom 12:14-16)

When someone does us wrong because of our faith in Jesus, it is called persecution. What should our attitude be toward our persecutors? It might feel like righteous indignation they have deserved to wish them harm, but God wants us to wish them their best future. When Jesus suffered during His arrest, trial and crucifixion, He could have called down twelve legions of angels (Matt 26:53). Yet, He did not. Instead, He prayed for them (Luke 23:34).

Peter wrote:
21 For even hereunto were ye called: because Christ also suffered for us, leaving us an example, that ye should follow his steps: 22 Who did no sin, neither was guile found in his

mouth: 23 Who, when he was reviled, reviled not again; when he suffered, he threatened not; but committed himself to him that judgeth righteously: (1 Peter 2:21-23)

Paul next wrote that we are to care for our brethren both in their triumphs and tragedies. When they rejoice, rejoice with them; when sorrow strikes, cry with them. Let their concerns be ours. He summed it up with these words, "Be of the same mind one toward another."

Then Paul tells us not to be snobs, keeping ourselves above other people, but to not be afraid of those who have less than us. Some years ago, I had an opportunity to volunteer in a ministry for teens in a troubled neighborhood where drive-by shootings would occur. As I pondered the distinct possibility of personal danger, I was reading here in Romans 12, and read, "Mind not high things, but condescend to men of low estate." To me, it was saying, don't be afraid to work, to "condescend", with these youth who, in my mind, could be considered "men of low estate." Yes, they lived in a troubled neighborhood, but I felt the Lord was saying to me, "Don't be afraid. Help them." And so reassured from the Lord, I did the volunteer work. The danger I feared never arose, either. So, the lesson here is, we should not consider ourselves so lofty or so wise that we can't work with people not as fortunate as ourselves.

17 Recompense to no man evil for evil. Provide things honest in the sight of all men. 18 If it be possible, as much as lieth in you, live peaceably with all men. 19 Dearly beloved, avenge not yourselves, but rather give place unto wrath: for it is written, Vengeance is mine; I will repay, saith the Lord. 20 Therefore if thine enemy hunger, feed him; if he thirst, give him drink: for in so doing thou shalt heap coals of fire on his head. 21 Be not overcome of evil, but overcome evil with good. (Rom

We just saw Peter's instruction about how Jesus did not retaliate against those who hurt Him, "because Christ also suffered for us, leaving us an example, that ye should follow his steps." Following in His steps, our Divine instruction about how we are to react to injustice suffered is that we are not to "pay people back" for what they have done wrongly to us. Evil done to us does NOT justify our turning around to do evil to someone else. We are to live doing honest things not evil.

So, what do we do if there is someone who wants to do injustice against us? Paul wrote in verse 18, "If it be possible, as much as lieth in you, live peaceably with all men." The first part of the command is "if it be possible." This is God recognizing that in some situation, it will not be possible. Nevertheless, in situations where it is possible, for our part we are to live peacefully with others, acknowledging that some people will not want to live peacefully with us. We can't control what other people's attitudes and actions will be. We are responsible for what ours will be.

Taking this further, what do we do if someone does do something wrong to us? We do not take revenge. Instead, we give it over to God, who has promised that He will take vengeance on them on our behalf. Give place to God in this matter, and His wrath will come against them! The words, "Vengeance is mine; I will repay, saith the Lord," are very powerful!

In the meantime, as we give place to God to let Him avenge us, what should we do to those who wrong us? The command given seems at first very strange. Paul writes, "20 Therefore if thine enemy hunger, feed him; if he thirst, give him drink: for in so doing thou shalt heap coals of fire on his head."

In the Sermon on the Mount, Jesus said,

44 But I say unto you, Love your enemies, bless them that curse you, do good to them that hate you, and pray for them which despitefully use you, and persecute you; (Matt 5:44-45)

We might say, wait, if I do good to them, it will drop flaming coals on their head? How is that overcoming evil with good? It sounds more like sending them to the fires of Hell.

We in the modern era have many conveniences of technology for starting fires. We just turn on our stove. But in those days, getting a fire going, say, a cooking fire, was not so easily done. What could happen back then (and I heard from a missionary that this actually still happens in some areas in the world today), is that a neighbor whose fire had gone out, would take a large clay pot or bowl, and balance it on their head, and come to you and ask for a live coal in the hopes of using it to restart their fire. If because of resentment for mistreatment that neighbor had done, we might say, well, okay, here is ONE coal, that coal might burn out before they returned to their home. Paul is teaching us that if our enemy comes to us in need, don't be stingy. Rather, be generous. Heap MANY coals in their clay pot, and so they carry on their head all those live coals with the happy guarantee they will get their fire restarted successfully.

We are to not pay back evil for evil, but to pay back goodness and kindness in return for evil suffered at their hands. In that way, we overcome evil with good. And really, this goes back to earlier in Romans 2 where Paul wrote:

4 Or despisest thou the riches of his goodness and forbearance and longsuffering; not knowing that the goodness of God leadeth thee to repentance? (Romans 2:4)

Just as God shows goodness (or kindness, in other translations) to us when we have done evil to Him, our being repaid good by God for our evil, works in our sinful hearts to lead us to repentance. As God has been good and kind to us, so we are to be good and kind to our fellow man.

Chapter 13
The Christian and Government

1 Let every soul be subject unto the higher powers. For there is no power but of God: the powers that be are ordained of God. 2 Whosoever therefore resisteth the power, resisteth the ordinance of God: and they that resist shall receive to themselves damnation. 3 For rulers are not a terror to good works, but to the evil. Wilt thou then not be afraid of the power? do that which is good, and thou shalt have praise of the same: 4 For he is the minister of God to thee for good. But if thou do that which is evil, be afraid; for he beareth not the sword in vain: for he is the minister of God, a revenger to execute wrath upon him that doeth evil. 5 Wherefore ye must needs be subject, not only for wrath, but also for conscience sake. (Rom 13:1-5)

Paul now addresses the role of the believer in relation to the government. Let us remember that the government of Paul's day (and of course, the days of the Roman believers to whom Paul was writing) was the government of Rome under the Roman Senate and of course, Caesar. Paul lets us know that whatever government is in power, God has ordained for that time and place in history. That means even a government of tyranny and despotism has its place in God's plans. While Rome had its time of infamy for persecuting Christians, yet the "Pax Romana" (Latin for the "[Peace in Rome]"), the peace that Rome enforced on all its territories, made possible the spread of the gospel to the four corners of the Roman Empire.

Paul tells us, under the inspiration of the Holy Spirit, that we as citizens are to be subject to our governments, whatever those may be. Paul wrote to his protégé Timothy about the need to pray for those in authority over us:

1 I exhort therefore, that, first of all, supplications, prayers, intercessions, and giving of thanks, be made for all men; 2 For kings, and for all that are in authority; that we may lead a quiet and peaceable life in all godliness and honesty. (1 Tim 2:1-2)

The important thing to remember is that God ordained the current government, and we are to live honestly and peaceably under it, doing good deeds. If we commit evil, God has authorized our government to bring wrath against us, though we are His believers. Peter also wrote about doing the right thing (not the wrong thing, for which we would get "buffeted"), including honoring the king (meaning the government):

17 Honour all men. Love the brotherhood. Fear God. Honour the king. 18 Servants, be subject to your masters with all fear; not only to the good and gentle, but also to the froward. 19 For this is thankworthy, if a man for conscience toward God endure grief, suffering wrongfully. 20 For what glory is it, if, when ye be buffeted for your faults, ye shall take it patiently? but if, when ye do well, and suffer for it, ye take it patiently, this is acceptable with God. (1 Peter 2:17-20)

Government's role is to be an agent for God to keep the peace and punish wrongdoing. The men and women in a government are agents for God, but when they abuse their authority and try to take upon themselves authority that which belongs to God only, then time may come for when a new government is necessary. In the days of the apostles, the governing authority in Jerusalem was the council of the Sanhedrin. It was supposed to oversee the people's spiritual wellbeing. Yet, it became an enemy of God by opposing the apostles who were preaching the gospel

.

26 Then went the captain with the officers, and brought them without violence: for they feared the people, lest they should have been stoned. 27 And when they had brought them, they set them before the council: and the high priest asked them, 28 Saying, Did not we straitly command you that ye should not teach in this name? and, behold, ye have filled Jerusalem with your doctrine, and intend to bring this man's blood upon us. 29 Then Peter and the other apostles answered and said, We ought to obey God rather than men. (Acts 5:26-29)

All things being said, we need to heed Paul's admonition, "Wherefore ye must needs be subject, not only for wrath, but also for conscience sake." What is at stake is not just obeying the government, but ultimately, it is about obeying God so as to have a clean conscience.

6 For for this cause pay ye tribute also: for they are God's ministers, attending continually upon this very thing. 7 Render therefore to all their dues: tribute to whom tribute is due; custom to whom custom; fear to whom fear; honour to whom honour. (Rom 13:6-7)

Taxes are never a delight and fun topic for people who have to pay them. Yet, they are how government agents get paid to be God's ministers of peacekeeping and punishment of evil. So, we are to render what is due them. Remember how Jesus was challenged about whether to pay taxes to Caesar?

16 And they sent out unto him their disciples with the Herodians, saying, Master, we know that thou art true, and teachest the way of God in truth, neither carest thou for any man: for thou regardest not the person of men. 17 Tell us therefore, What thinkest thou? Is it lawful to give tribute unto Caesar, or not? 18 But Jesus perceived their wickedness, and said, Why tempt ye me, ye hypocrites? 19 Shew me the tribute money. And they brought unto him a penny. 20 And he saith unto them, Whose is this image and superscription? 21 They say unto him, Caesar's. Then saith he unto them, Render therefore unto Caesar the things which are Caesar's; and unto God the things that are God's. 22 When they had heard these words, they marvelled, and left him, and went their way. (Matt 22:16-22)

When Jesus was challenged about whether He would pay the required tax, here is what happened:

24 And when they were come to Capernaum, they that received tribute money came to Peter, and said, Doth not your master pay tribute? 25 He saith, Yes. And when he was come into the house, Jesus prevented him, saying, What thinkest thou, Simon? of whom do the kings of the earth take custom or tribute? of their own children, or of strangers? 26 Peter saith unto him, Of strangers. Jesus saith unto him, Then are the children free. 27 Notwithstanding, lest we should offend them, go thou to the sea, and cast an hook, and take up the fish that first cometh up; and when thou hast opened his mouth, thou shalt find a piece of money: that take, and give unto them for me and thee. (Matt 17:24-27)

So, we need to render unto Caesar that which is Caesar's, including respecting and honoring the representatives of the government.

8 Owe no man any thing, but to love one another: for he that loveth another hath fulfilled the law. 9 For this, Thou shalt not commit adultery, Thou shalt not kill, Thou shalt not steal, Thou shalt not bear false witness, Thou shalt not covet; and if there be any other commandment, it is briefly comprehended in this saying, namely, Thou shalt love thy neighbour as thyself. 10 Love worketh no ill to his neighbour: therefore love is the fulfilling of the law. (Rom 13:8-10)

Paul expands upon his list of things to do in relation to the government where he had said that we should not owe "fear" or "honor", or "custom" or "tribute", and says to go beyond those and "Owe no man any thing." There is one exception, though. We owe it to others, as born-again believers in Jesus Christ, to love one another. That is a "debt" we can never "pay off." The love we are to owe one another is the Greek ἀγαπάω agapaō, otherwise called "agape" love which means "to welcome, to entertain, to be fond of, to love dearly." Fellow believers are to be loved dearly! Agape love is a love that gives without a hidden agenda looking for any kind of a payback in return. It is given with the best intentions of another's wellbeing.

When we love one another like that, it fulfills the law. We won't commit adultery, murder, steal, lie or covet, or do any other unkind or wrongful thing. When we love like that, we are seeking someone else's best interests, and will not work any wrong of any kind against them.
Agape is ultimately the kind of love that God has for us.

16 For God so loved [ἀγαπάω agapaō] the world, that he gave his only begotten Son, that whosoever believeth in him should not perish, but have everlasting life. (John 3:16)

1 Behold, what manner of love [ἀγάπη agapē] the Father hath bestowed upon us, that we should be called the sons of God: therefore the world knoweth us not, because it knew him not. (1 John 3:1)
[ἀγαπάω agapaō] is the verb form of "love"; [ἀγάπη agapē] is the noun form of "love"

11 And that, knowing the time, that now it is high time to awake out of sleep: for now is our salvation nearer than when we believed. 12 The night is far spent, the day is at hand: let us therefore cast off the works of darkness, and let us put on the armour of light. (Rom 13:11-12)

After encouraging us to always love each other, Paul reminds us that prophecy moves on. Every day draws us closer to the time when Christ will resurrect us in the Rapture (1 Thes 4:16-18). Let us be determined to be about our Lord's business. Let us not be "asleep at the wheel," for the Lord's coming draws closer every day.

1 But of the times and the seasons, brethren, ye have no need that I write unto you. 2 For yourselves know perfectly that the day of the Lord so cometh as a thief in the night. 3 For when they shall say, Peace and safety; then sudden destruction cometh upon them, as travail upon a woman with child; and they shall not escape. 4 But ye, brethren, are not in darkness, that that day should overtake you as a thief. 5 Ye are all the children of light, and the children of the day: we are not of the night, nor of darkness. 6 Therefore let us not

sleep, as do others; but let us watch and be sober. 7 For they that sleep sleep in the night; and they that be drunken are drunken in the night. 8 But let us, who are of the day, be sober, putting on the breastplate of faith and love; and for an helmet, the hope of salvation. 9 For God hath not appointed us to wrath, but to obtain salvation by our Lord Jesus Christ (1 Thes 5:1-9)

Knowing that we want to be found by Jesus doing good, not evil, Paul tells us "let us therefore cast off the works of darkness." Turn away from sin and instead embrace the good. We are told, "and let us put on the armour of light."

In his letter to the Ephesians, Paul speaks of the armor we are to wear.

10 Finally, my brethren, be strong in the Lord, and in the power of his might. 11 Put on the whole armour of God, that ye may be able to stand against the wiles of the devil. 12 For we wrestle not against flesh and blood, but against principalities, against powers, against the rulers of the darkness of this world, against spiritual wickedness in high places. 13 Wherefore take unto you the whole armour of God, that ye may be able to withstand in the evil day, and having done all, to stand. 14 Stand therefore, having your loins girt about with truth, and having on the breastplate of righteousness; 15 And your feet shod with the preparation of the gospel of peace; 16 Above all, taking the shield of faith, wherewith ye shall be able to quench all the fiery darts of the wicked. 17 And take the helmet of salvation, and the sword of the Spirit, which is the word of God (Eph 6:10-17)

God has supplied the equipment – it is up to us to put it on and use it.

13 Let us walk honestly, as in the day; not in rioting and drunkenness, not in chambering and wantonness, not in strife and envying. 14 But put ye on the Lord Jesus Christ, and make not provision for the flesh, to fulfil the lusts thereof. (Rom 13:13-14)

The archaic words of the King James Version Bible need some explanation. "Rioting" is not the action of a mob angry over a perceived injustice, with overturning cars and breaking windows and such. Rather, it is the Greek κῶμος kōmos which means:

"a revel, carousal, a nocturnal and riotous procession of half drunken and frolicsome fellows who after supper parade through the streets with torches and music in honour of Bacchus or some other deity, and sing and play before houses of male and female friends; hence used generally of feasts and drinking parties that are protracted till late at night and indulge in revelry."

Drunkenness is, of course, self-explanatory. The next word, "chambering", is strange to 21st century ears. It is the Greek κοίτη koitē and means the bed chamber, or room, where sexual sin can be practiced, such as between two cohabiting people, a boyfriend and girlfriend living together and having sex even though they are not married.

The next word, wantonness, is the Greek ἀσέλγεια aselgeia which means "unbridled lust, excess, licentiousness, lasciviousness, wantonness, outrageousness, shamelessness, insolence." This should raise a red flag for us who believe. It is saying that this is how we should NOT live, but it implies that is possible that a believer CAN live that way. It should serve as warning that we be not proud and think, Oh, I could never fall into THAT kind of sin. God forbid, but, Yes, we can!

Scripture speaks to the Corinthians who had a problem with sexual immorality in their midst, and Paul warned them.

6 Now these things were our examples, to the intent we should not lust after evil things, as they also lusted. 7 Neither be ye idolaters, as were some of them; as it is written, The people sat down to eat and drink, and rose up to play. 8 Neither let us commit fornication, as some of them committed, and fell in one day three and twenty thousand. 9 Neither let us tempt Christ, as some of them also tempted, and were destroyed of serpents. 10 Neither murmur ye, as some of them also murmured, and were destroyed of the destroyer. 11 Now all these things happened unto them for examples: and they are written for our admonition, upon whom the ends of the world are come. 12 Wherefore let him that thinketh he standeth take heed lest he fall. (1 Cor 10:6-12)

Paul's warning is that, if we as believers should give in to unbridled lust, that is, ἀσέλγεια aselgeia, we can also expect that God may have to deal harshly with us in judgment, perhaps even to go so far as to take us home before our time as He did with the ancient Israelites. This is not to say we would lose our salvation. No, never that. But, we might lose our life. As long as we live in these mortal bodies, we will still sin. God is patient and longsuffering, slow to anger and quick to forgive. It is best to confess and forsake sin, even as the Scripture says:

31 For if we would judge ourselves, we should not be judged. 32 But when we are judged, we are chastened of the Lord, that we should not be condemned with the world. (1 Cor 11:31-32)

Paul's next two words are "strife" and "envying." Strife is the Greek word ἔρις eris which simply means, arguments or quarreling. Envying is the Greek word ζῆλος zēlos from which we get the words "zeal," "zealous" and "zealot." It can be used both in a favorable sense, and unhappily, in an unfavorable sense, which is the case here in Romans 13:13. Both are wrongful behavior for us as Christians to be engaged in.

Paul also has warned about this kind of misbehavior here:

20 For I fear, lest, when I come, I shall not find you such as I would, and that I shall be found unto you such as ye would not: lest there be debates, envyings, wraths, strifes, backbitings, whisperings, swellings, tumults (2 Cor 12:20)

So, what is the solution for all these things against which Paul is warning the Romans (and through them, us today)? He simply states, "But put ye on the Lord Jesus Christ, and make not provision for the flesh, to fulfil the lusts thereof." The words "put ye on" are from the Greek ἐνδύω endyō, which means simply enough, "to sink into (clothing), put on, clothe one's self." We are to wear the Lord Jesus as if He were our clothing. Indeed, He is also our armor, in which we saw earlier that we are to clothe ourselves.

How do we do that? There was a classic book written in the 1800s called, "In His Steps" by Charles M Sheldon. The simple message of the book is this: ""What would Jesus do?" When members of an ordinary American church are challenged to not take a single action without first asking themselves that simple question, their lives, their congregation, and their community are transformed."

This expression, what would Jesus do, even became a fad among teenagers who abbreviated it as WWJD? To put on, or clothe ourselves, with the Lord Jesus Christ would be to consider first, what would Jesus do? Would He do this, or that?

The way to put on Jesus is given by Paul: "make not provision for the flesh, to fulfil the lusts thereof." For instance, if we have a problem with alcohol, don't rent a room over a bar. There are many ways to apply this. We can discern what is appropriate by asking ourselves, What would Jesus do?

Chapter 14

1 Him that is weak in the faith receive ye, but not to doubtful disputations. 2 For one believeth that he may eat all things: another, who is weak, eateth herbs. 3 Let not him that eateth despise him that eateth not; and let not him which eateth not judge him that eateth: for God hath received him. 4 Who art thou that judgest another man's servant? to his own master he standeth or falleth. Yea, he shall be holden up: for God is able to make him stand. 5 One man esteemeth one day above another: another esteemeth every day alike. Let every man be fully persuaded in his own mind. (Rom 14:1-5)

As comprehensive as God's Word is, there are areas of life that not specifically addressed in Scripture. These are commonly called "gray areas," and in themselves are morally neutral, being neither right nor wrong. However, they can become right or wrong based on how they are believed and treated. For the believers in Rome, one such gray area was the matter of food and drink. The Romans had many false gods. The Greeks originally invented many "gods", Zeus, Heracles, Apollo, Aphrodite, and many others. When the Romans conquered Greece, they took the entire pantheon of those Greek gods and "Romanized" them by renaming them. Zeus became Jupiter, Heracles became Hercules, Aphrodite became Venus, and so on.

Temples in Rome were dedicated to the worship of those Greco-Roman gods. One of things done in those temple services was to sacrifice an animal to the appropriate deity, and then when it was all over, they took the carcass of the animal and sold it as meat in the market. Likewise, wine was offered to the false gods, and then the rest sold at market.

The "gray area" that came about for new Christians in Rome was a determination to keep their distance from the false gods they formerly worshiped. So, they dreaded the meat and drink offered to those false gods, believing that to eat and drink such would be considered a participation in the idol worship associated with the food and drink. To those believers, eating and drinking such would be a sin because those items had been offered to those false gods.

Other "gray areas" included the matter of Saturday being a no-work Sabbath day, and whether to celebrate certain holidays the Romans had instituted.

Where a believer stood on these "gray areas" has become known in theological terms as the weaker brother/stronger brother. In essence, if a person felt they would be committing a sin by eating or drinking, then they are the weaker brother because their conscience is weak in that area. They are considering something to be sin which is NOT sin in itself. The one who has the clear conscience to eat such meat and drink is the stronger brother.

So, how do we handle these "gray areas"? Paul's instruction, inspired by the Holy Spirit, is that we make allowances for each other. He wrote, "Let not him that eateth despise him that eateth not..." The stronger brother is the one who eats. The temptation for him is to "despise" a weaker brother in Christ who has not got the freedom in his conscience to eat like he (the stronger brother) does. Paul is saying, "Don't you dare look down on your brother in this matter!" Do not despise him!

Then, Paul addresses the weaker brother, "… and let not him which eateth not judge him that eateth: for God hath received him." To such a one, Paul is saying, "Don't you dare accuse of sin the one who has the clear conscience to eat!" Do not judge him!

Why such instructions? Because they are needed for these "gray areas" that are not specifically addressed in Scripture. Each person should be convinced according to his conscience.

6 He that regardeth the day, regardeth it unto the Lord; and he that regardeth not the day, to the Lord he doth not regard it. He that eateth, eateth to the Lord, for he giveth God thanks; and he that eateth not, to the Lord he eateth not, and giveth God thanks. 7 For none of us liveth to himself, and no man dieth to himself. 8 For whether we live, we live unto the Lord; and whether we die, we die unto the Lord: whether we live therefore, or die, we are the Lord's. 9 For to this end Christ both died, and rose, and revived, that he might be Lord both of the dead and living. (Rom 14:6-9)

Paul now gives God-honoring practical examples of how to handle "gray areas." If someone feels a day needs special attention, then for him it is to be done as for the Lord. On the other hand, if a person sees no special need for observance of a particular day, let him do that as unto the Lord. The same thing applies to eating. The one who has no qualms about eating certain foods eats it, giving thanks for that food. However, on the other hand, if someone has an issue with certain foods, then don't eat those foods, and just give thanks to God the food he can with good conscience eat.

In the end, whether we live or die, which encompasses all of life, whether eating foods or celebrating certain days, our goal, focus and purpose needs to be honoring God in all we do. Paul wrote to the Corinthians:

31 Whether therefore ye eat, or drink, or whatsoever ye do, do all to the glory of God. (1 Cor 10:31)

In life and in death, let us remember that we belong to the Lord Jesus Christ, who purchased our freedom with His blood shed on Calvary's cross.

10 But why dost thou judge thy brother? or why dost thou set at nought thy brother? for we shall all stand before the judgment seat of Christ. 11 For it is written, As I live, saith the Lord, every knee shall bow to me, and every tongue shall confess to God. 12 So then every one of us shall give account of himself to God. 13 Let us not therefore judge one another any more: but judge this rather, that no man put a stumblingblock or an occasion to fall in his brother's way. (Rom 14:10-13)

Going back to what he wrote earlier about the weaker brother/stronger brother, Paul warns about how we treat our brothers and sisters in Christ in regard to "gray areas." He asks, "Why dost thou judge thy brother?" The question is directed at the weaker brother, that is, the person who thinks he cannot eat certain foods or has to be careful to observe certain days. If that person sees someone exercising freedom to eat foods which he cannot in good conscience eat, that person is not to say the one who eats is committing sin. Do not judge!

Then Paul addresses the stronger brother, saying, "Why dost thou set at nought thy brother?" That is to say, the one who has the freedom to eat should not look down in contempt on the brother who does not have the freedom of conscience to eat, nor should he despise that person's weakness.

The reasons for why we avoid both extremes of judging nor despising, is that we ALL have to stand before the judgment seat of Christ to give an account of ourselves. It is not our place to weigh and evaluate a brother or sister's worth to God. That is reserved for the Lord Jesus Christ alone.

There is, however, one area where we are to judge. We are to put no stumbling block before our brother or sister in Christ. What is a stumbling block? It is something so small that it hardly is obvious as we walk along in the path, and because it is not some big and weighty thing, we do not notice it. Yet, it can catch our toe and trip us. The application of this idea is that the "gray areas" for the stronger brother/weaker brother are NOT all that big a deal. They are NOT some big and weighty matter, but are small things, and we should not trip each other up with these sorts of things!

14 I know, and am persuaded by the Lord Jesus, that there is nothing unclean of itself: but to him that esteemeth any thing to be unclean, to him it is unclean. 15 But if thy brother be grieved with thy meat, now walkest thou not charitably. Destroy not him with thy meat, for whom Christ died. 16 Let not then your good be evil spoken of: 17 For the kingdom of God is not meat and drink; but righteousness, and peace, and joy in the Holy Ghost. 18 For he that in these things serveth Christ is

acceptable to God, and approved of men. (Rom 14:14-18)

Paul then gives assurance that there really is no problem with any meat being "unclean" of itself. It is not a sacrilege nor a sin to eat meat that was sacrificed to idols. However, until a weaker brother or sister learns this and takes it to heart, if they feel certain foods are unclean, then for them it IS unclean and therefore it would be a violation of their earnest conscience. If they ate, they would feel guilty as if they had sinned against the Lord.

A potential problem lies in waiting for the stronger brother. When Paul wrote, "destroy not him with thy meat, for whom Christ died," he was warning the stronger brother not to exercise his freedom to eat before a weaker brother, if by doing so he encouraged the weaker to go ahead and eat what he has no clear conscience to eat. Be sensitive about their weakness, so as to not cause them to stumble. The kingdom of God is not about eating and drinking (or NOT eating or drinking). Righteousness, peace and joy are what the kingdom of God is about through the Holy Spirit Who indwells every believer.

19 Let us therefore follow after the things which make for peace, and things wherewith one may edify another. 20 For meat destroy not the work of God. All things indeed are pure; but it is evil for that man who eateth with offence. 21 It is good neither to eat flesh, nor to drink wine, nor any thing whereby thy brother stumbleth, or is offended, or is made weak. 22 Hast thou faith? have it to thyself before God. Happy is he that condemneth not himself in that thing which he alloweth. 23 And he that doubteth is damned if he eat, because he

eateth not of faith: for whatsoever is not of faith is sin. (Rom 14:19-23)

With the understandings that righteousness, peace and joy are what the Kingdom of God is all about, we need to love our brothers and sisters in the Lord and not tear one another down with non-essential things like whether or not we can eat or drink something. Let's pursue peace and build one another up. Applying this to the "gray areas", it is important that the stronger brother look out for the weaker brother. Don't encourage them to go against their conscience! Paul sternly says, "Hast thou faith? have it to thyself before God." In other words, keep your freedom to yourself and do not flaunt it in the weaker brother's face, tempting them to violate their conscience! It should be the stronger brother's motivation that he do this out of love for the weaker brother.

In earthly families, the bigger brother out of love goes to the defense of his little brother, protecting him from bullies. Should not the stronger brother in Christ so love his weaker brother to protect him from violating his conscience by not flaunting his freedom to eat and drink, a freedom the weaker brother does not have?

Paul has final words for the two.

To the stronger brother he writes, "Happy is he that condemneth not himself in that thing which he alloweth." Don't allow his freedom to bring condemnation on himself for putting a stumbling block before a weaker brother to eat against his conscience.

To the weaker brother, Paul writes, "And he that doubteth is damned if he eat, because he eateth not of faith." The word "damned" is not talking about the eternal damnation of Hell, but is simply talking about how violating our conscience brings guilt of sin.

How can eating something that is not actually sinful, bring about the guilt of sin? Pal concludes the chapter by simply saying, "for whatsoever is not of faith is sin."

While the examples of this chapter were about eating and drinking, this principle applies to ANY "gray area" of our lives, whether it is attending a sporting event or doing laundry on Sunday. If we do not have a clear conscience to do something, whatever it is, then for us, it WILL be sin!

Chapter 15

1 We then that are strong ought to bear the infirmities of the weak, and not to please ourselves. 2 Let every one of us please his neighbour for his good to edification. 3 For even Christ pleased not himself; but, as it is written, The reproaches of them that reproached thee fell on me. (Rom 15:1-3)

It is the standard of Biblical agape love that we look out for one another's welfare.

4 Look not every man on his own things, but every man also on the things of others. (Phil 2:4)

However, that is not quite Paul's meaning in Rom 15:1 when he writes for us to "bear the infirmities of the weak". The Greek word for "infirmities" is ἀσθένημα asthenēma, which means "of error arising from weakness of mind." In other words, Paul is still talking about the weaker brother/stronger brother issue. Those who have strong faith have to bear with those who are weak in their faith, meaning, those who think a non-sinful thing is sinful. The strong are to be patient and accommodating with the weaker brother, and are not to merely think only of themselves, i.e. "please ourselves." The Greek ἀρέσκω areskō for "please" means "to accommodate one's self to the opinions desires and interests of others." Why? Because if we are acting in agape love, we will seek to build one another up, and if we have to make allowances for our weaker brother's faulty understanding of "gray areas", then make those allowances out of love for them.

As is true in every area of the Christian life, Jesus is our role model for how we are to not "please" ourselves, even as He did not please Himself. The almighty Son of God full of grace and glory humbled Himself and took on the form of a human being as a man, being born in a manger in Bethlehem. He hungered and thirsted like we do, and grew tired and weary, just as we do. He accommodated Himself with our overall weakness, and as a result, He was reproached by self-righteous people.

16 But whereunto shall I liken this generation? It is like unto children sitting in the markets, and calling unto their fellows, 17 And saying, We have piped unto you, and ye have not danced; we have mourned unto you, and ye have not lamented. 18 For John came neither eating nor drinking, and they say, He hath a devil. 19 The Son of man came eating and drinking, and they say, Behold a man gluttonous, and a winebibber, a friend of publicans and sinners. But wisdom is justified of her children. (Matt 11:16-19)

How gracious He is, that He would do that for you and me!

4 For whatsoever things were written aforetime were written for our learning, that we through patience and comfort of the scriptures might have hope. 5 Now the God of patience and consolation grant you to be likeminded one toward another according to Christ Jesus: 6 That ye may with one mind and one mouth glorify God, even the Father of our Lord Jesus Christ. 7 Wherefore receive ye one another, as Christ also received us to the glory of God. (Rom 15:4-7)

How we as Christians treat each other finds its roots in the Old Testament, for if someone treated others with love, it was a fulfillment of the law.

10 Love worketh no ill to his neighbour: therefore love is the fulfilling of the law. (Rom 13:10)

When it comes to brothers and sisters in the faith, whether it is regard to a weaker brother/stronger brother situation, or whatever differences we have, we have in the Scriptures the reasons we can be patient with one another, and there is consolation, too. Paul urges us to be like-minded, for if we all treat each other with agape love, then our differences won't really be all that important. When we do this, then we glorify God.

31 Whether therefore ye eat, or drink, or whatsoever ye do, do all to the glory of God. (1 Cor 10:31)

Paul says for us to receive one another, just in the same way that God receives us in Christ.

8 Now I say that Jesus Christ was a minister of the circumcision for the truth of God, to confirm the promises made unto the fathers: 9 And that the Gentiles might glorify God for his mercy; as it is written, For this cause I will confess to thee among the Gentiles, and sing unto thy name. 10 And again he saith, Rejoice, ye Gentiles, with his people. 11 And again, Praise the Lord, all ye Gentiles; and laud him, all ye people. 12 And again, Esaias saith, There shall be a root of Jesse, and he that shall rise to reign over the Gentiles; in him shall the Gentiles trust. (Rom 15:8-12)

Having told the Romans (and us) that we are to be like-minded, Paul reminds us that Jesus came originally for the children of Israel, whom he called "the circumcision". Jesus acknowledged that purpose for His coming:

21 Then Jesus went thence, and departed into the coasts of Tyre and Sidon. 22 And, behold, a woman of Canaan came out of the same coasts, and cried unto him, saying, Have mercy on me, O Lord, thou son of David; my daughter is grievously vexed with a devil. 23 But he answered her not a word. And his disciples came and besought him, saying, Send her away; for she crieth after us. 24 But he answered and said, I am not sent but unto the lost sheep of the house of Israel. (Matt 18:21-24)

But because of the Gentile woman's faith, He granted what she asked and healed the woman's daughter.

So, what we see is that though Jesus came for the children of Israel, yet His salvation became available to Gentiles as well. The common denominator is our faith in Him.

13 Now the God of hope fill you with all joy and peace in believing, that ye may abound in hope, through the power of the Holy Ghost. 14 And I myself also am persuaded of you, my brethren, that ye also are full of goodness, filled with all knowledge, able also to admonish one another. 15 Nevertheless, brethren, I have written the more boldly unto you in some sort, as putting you in mind, because of the grace that is given to me of God, 16 That I should be the minister of Jesus Christ to the Gentiles, ministering the gospel of God, that the offering up of the Gentiles might be acceptable, being sanctified by the Holy Ghost. (Romans 15:13-16)

God is the God of hope! He so graciously brings salvation to all who will believe, whether a Jew (the circumcision) or a Gentile (the Romans and the rest of us). With that hope He gives, we have peace and joy. We have believed and we are forgiven and going to Heaven! Hell is no longer an option! The grave is not the end. The Holy Spirit has been given to us, and we find the power to live for God through Him. We learn God's ways, and admonish, encourage and love one another. Paul speaks of his calling to be a minister of the gospel of God's grace to the Gentiles.

17 I have therefore whereof I may glory through Jesus Christ in those things which pertain to God. 18 For I will not dare to speak of any of those things which Christ hath not wrought by me, to make the Gentiles obedient, by word and deed, 19 Through mighty signs and wonders, by the power of the Spirit of God; so that from Jerusalem, and round about unto Illyricum, I have fully preached the gospel of Christ. 20 Yea, so have I strived to preach the gospel, not where Christ was named, lest I should build upon another man's foundation: 21 But as it is written, To whom he was not spoken of, they shall see: and they that have not heard shall understand. (Rom 15:17-21)

Paul's desire was to give glory to God. He wanted glory to go to God for the things God has done, but no glory for himself. He wrote to the Corinthians:

31 Whether therefore ye eat, or drink, or whatsoever ye do, do all to the glory of God. (1 Cor 10:31)

He had been commissioned by Jesus to go to the Gentiles to

preach Christ, and that was ever in his mind and heart to do that. God used Paul to work "mighty signs and wonders" by the power of the Holy Spirit.

10 And this continued by the space of two years; so that all they which dwelt in Asia heard the word of the Lord Jesus, both Jews and Greeks. 11 And God wrought special miracles by the hands of Paul: 12 So that from his body were brought unto the sick handkerchiefs or aprons, and the diseases departed from them, and the evil spirits went out of them. (Acts 19:10-12)

Paul's driving energy was to break new ground, not to preach where someone else had already gone, for he wanted to be the one laying a foundation in Christ in the lives and hearts of people.

22 For which cause also I have been much hindered from coming to you. 23 But now having no more place in these parts, and having a great desire these many years to come unto you; 24 Whensoever I take my journey into Spain, I will come to you: for I trust to see you in my journey, and to be brought on my way thitherward by you, if first I be somewhat filled with your company. 25 But now I go unto Jerusalem to minister unto the saints. 26 For it hath pleased them of Macedonia and Achaia to make a certain contribution for the poor saints which are at Jerusalem. 27 It hath pleased them verily; and their debtors they are. For if the Gentiles have been made partakers of their spiritual things, their duty is also to minister unto them in carnal things. 28 When therefore I have performed this, and have sealed to them this fruit, I will come by you into Spain. 29 And I am sure that, when

I come unto you, I shall come in the fulness of the blessing of the gospel of Christ. 30 Now I beseech you, brethren, for the Lord Jesus Christ's sake, and for the love of the Spirit, that ye strive together with me in your prayers to God for me; 31 That I may be delivered from them that do not believe in Judaea; and that my service which I have for Jerusalem may be accepted of the saints; 32 That I may come unto you with joy by the will of God, and may with you be refreshed. 33 Now the God of peace be with you all. Amen. (Rom 15:22-33)

Paul wanted to come to the believers in the great city of Rime, the capital of the known world. Yet, God hindered him, and as a result, Paul had to write this letter to the Romans, by which believers down through all the centuries since have had as a teaching resource for the things Christians have needed to know about God, Christ, and the gospel of God's grace. Even with the writing of this letter, Paul still desired to come and see them personally, but other things required his presence elsewhere. Gentiles had received immense spiritual blessings through the children of Israel, for it was through Israel that Jesus came and that the Scriptures were written and preserved, and so it was fitting for these Gentiles who had been saved by the preaching of the gospel to minister to the needs of their spiritual brethren.

One such thing was the freewill offering of "them of Macedonia and Achaia" for the needs of believers in Jerusalem. Though Paul had a commission to preach to the Gentiles, he still cared for the welfare of believing Jews back home in Jerusalem.

Finally, Paul asked for prayer, as he often did.

3 Withal praying also for us, that God would open unto us a door of utterance, to speak the mystery of Christ, for which I am also in bonds: (Col 4:3)

25 Brethren, pray for us. (1 Thes 5:25)

3 Finally, brethren, pray for us, that the word of the Lord may have free course, and be glorified, even as it is with you: (2 Thes 3:1)

Ultimately, we are to pray, pray, pray.
17 Pray without ceasing. (1 Thes 5:17)

Chapter 16

1 I commend unto you Phebe our sister, which is a servant of the church which is at Cenchrea: 2 That ye receive her in the Lord, as becometh saints, and that ye assist her in whatsoever business she hath need of you: for she hath been a succourer of many, and of myself also. 3 Greet Priscilla and Aquila my helpers in Christ Jesus: 4 Who have for my life laid down their own necks: unto whom not only I give thanks, but also all the churches of the Gentiles. 5 Likewise greet the church that is in their house. Salute my wellbeloved Epaenetus, who is the firstfruits of Achaia unto Christ. 6 Greet Mary, who bestowed much labour on us. 7 Salute Andronicus and Junia, my kinsmen, and my fellowprisoners, who are of note among the apostles, who also were in Christ before me. 8 Greet Amplias my beloved in the Lord. 9 Salute Urbane, our helper in Christ, and Stachys my beloved. 10 Salute Apelles approved in Christ. Salute them which are of Aristobulus' household. 11 Salute Herodion my kinsman. Greet them that be of the household of Narcissus, which are in the Lord. 12 Salute Tryphena and Tryphosa, who labour in the Lord. Salute the beloved Persis, which laboured much in the Lord. 13 Salute Rufus chosen in the Lord, and his mother and mine. 14 Salute Asyncritus, Phlegon, Hermas, Patrobas, Hermes, and the brethren which are with them. 15 Salute Philologus, and Julia, Nereus, and his sister, and Olympas, and all the saints which are with them. 16 Salute one another with an holy kiss. The churches of Christ salute you. (Rom 16:1-15)

As Paul concludes his letter to the Romans, he names many believers, giving each a personal greeting. Now, the Roman

Catholic Church has made the claim that Peter was the first pope, and that he presided as pope from Rome. Yet, despite all the individual names Paul addresses, he does not ever name Peter, which would have been an incredible omission. The truth is, Peter was NOT in Rome, nor in authority there. That claim by the Roman Catholic Church is spurious (i.e. not being what it purports to be; false or fake.)

17 Now I beseech you, brethren, mark them which cause divisions and offences contrary to the doctrine which ye have learned; and avoid them. 18 For they that are such serve not our Lord Jesus Christ, but their own belly; and by good words and fair speeches deceive the hearts of the simple. 19 For your obedience is come abroad unto all men. I am glad therefore on your behalf: but yet I would have you wise unto that which is good, and simple concerning evil. 20 And the God of peace shall bruise Satan under your feet shortly. The grace of our Lord Jesus Christ be with you. Amen.

Paul then gives a final instruction to watch out for false teachers and avoid them. A similar warning was given by Peter:

1 But there were false prophets also among the people, even as there shall be false teachers among you, who privily shall bring in damnable heresies, even denying the Lord that bought them, and bring upon themselves swift destruction. 2 And many shall follow their pernicious ways; by reason of whom the way of truth shall be evil spoken of. 3 And through covetousness shall they with feigned words make merchandise of you: whose judgment now of a long time

lingereth not, and their damnation slumbereth not. (2 Peter 2:1-3)

21 Timotheus my workfellow, and Lucius, and Jason, and Sosipater, my kinsmen, salute you. 22 I Tertius, who wrote this epistle, salute you in the Lord. 23 Gaius mine host, and of the whole church, saluteth you. Erastus the chamberlain of the city saluteth you, and Quartus a brother. 24 The grace of our Lord Jesus Christ be with you all. Amen. 25 Now to him that is of power to stablish you according to my gospel, and the preaching of Jesus Christ, according to the revelation of the mystery, which was kept secret since the world began, 26 But now is made manifest, and by the scriptures of the prophets, according to the commandment of the everlasting God, made known to all nations for the obedience of faith: 27 To God only wise, be glory through Jesus Christ for ever. Amen. (Rom 16:21-27)

The letter to the Romans is truly about the grace of God revealed in the gospel. What is amazing is that Paul tells us that the gospel "was kept secret since the world began." The gospel was not a "last minute" effort by God to save people, but He had planned it all along since the Creation of the world. It is only in these New Testament times that it was finally revealed. But, if that is the case, why did He bother with the giving of the Law to Moses and the children of Israel? Why didn't He just give us the gospel?

The answer lies in what Jesus said:

17 When Jesus heard it, he saith unto them, They that are whole have no need of the physician, but they that are sick: I

came not to call the righteous, but sinners to repentance. (Mark 2:17)

A person won't seek the help of a physician if he does not believe he is sick. It is through the Law that we learned how sinful sin really is, and therefore how desperately we need to be saved from it. The Law itself could never save us, as it only condemns us. Thinking of Jesus's words above, the Law came in to inform us that we ARE "sick" and need the "Great Physician", Jesus Himself, to save us from the fatal spiritual disease that is sin. This is illustrated in one of the events in the history of the children of Israel.

5 And the people spake against God, and against Moses, Wherefore have ye brought us up out of Egypt to die in the wilderness? for there is no bread, neither is there any water; and our soul loatheth this light bread. 6 And the LORD sent fiery serpents among the people, and they bit the people; and much people of Israel died. 7 Therefore the people came to Moses, and said, We have sinned, for we have spoken against the LORD, and against thee; pray unto the LORD, that he take away the serpents from us. And Moses prayed for the people. 8 And the LORD said unto Moses, Make thee a fiery serpent, and set it upon a pole: and it shall come to pass, that every one that is bitten, when he looketh upon it, shall live. 9 And Moses made a serpent of brass, and put it upon a pole, and it came to pass, that if a serpent had bitten any man, when he beheld the serpent of brass, he lived. (Numbers 21:5-9)

The Israelites complained against God, and He sent the serpents to smite them in judgment against them in their sin. They quickly realized they were in trouble, and cried out to

Moses to intercede for them. God's response was a picture of Christ on the cross. He told them to make out of brass metal an image of the serpents and put it on the top of a pole. If anyone was bitten, they had but to believe God that they should look up at God's provision and they would be saved.

In this illustration, the snake bite's poison is a picture of the sin that is killing us all. God's provision is Christ Jesus on a cross at Calvary where He bore our sins, in fact, where Scripture says He was made sin for us.

21 For he hath made him to be sin for us, who knew no sin; that we might be made the righteousness of God in him. (2 Cor 5:21)

Being made sin (pictured by the serpent on the pole), Christ was raised up on the cross. If anyone wants to be saved from sin, they need but look up at God's provision of Jesus Christ on Calvary cross, and they would be saved. Please notice that the response, to look to Jesus on the cross, is purely one of faith with no works, and that provision for salvation for sinners is made freely available by God's amazing grace.

Finally, Paul closes with praise for God and for Jesus Christ. Amen!

Made in the USA
Las Vegas, NV
06 May 2022

48497641R00100